"Above all, it is imperative to eliminate the idea that any fantastic, mysterious practices are required for the attainment of higher knowledge. It must be clearly realized that a start has to be made with the thoughts and feelings with which we continually live, and that these feelings and thoughts must merely be given a new direction. Everyone must say to himself: "In my own world of thought and feeling the deepest mysteries lie hidden, only until now I have been unable to perceive them."

— Rudolf Steiner

*"Every object, well-contemplated,
creates an organ of perception in us."*

— Johann Wolfgang von Goethe

To Sue —
may you find
gifts of wisdom
every day —
Lynn Jericho
2018

INNER CHRISTMAS
every day

BOOK ONE

YOUR SOUL'S

12 PERCEPTIONS: THE GIFTS OF PERCEIVING

12 PREPOSITIONS: THE GIFTS OF RELATING

12 QUALITIES: THE GIFTS OF CHARACTERIZING

12 POLARITIES: THE GIFTS OF BALANCING

Gifts from the Twelve Holy Nights

LYNN JERICHO

Inner Christmas Everyday
Gifts from the Twelve Holy Nights

Book One:

Your Soul's 12...
Perceptions
Prepositions
Qualities
Polarities

Copyright 2017 Lynn Jericho. All rights reserved.
No part of this book may be reproduced or transmitted in any form, by any means, (electronic, photocopying, recording, or otherwise) without the prior written permission of the publisher.

Cover and book design by Lee Hannam at yellowfishdesign.co.uk

an Imagine Self publication
www.imagineself.com

ISBN 978-0-9993644-0-6

If you do not understand something and need some clarification, please email me.
Lynn Jericho

INNER CHRISTMAS
every day
THE BOOK SERIES

BOOK ONE
YOUR SOUL'S
12 PERCEPTIONS
12 PREPOSITIONS
12 QUALITIES
12 POLARITIES

BOOK TWO
YOUR SOUL'S
12 NEEDS
12 INTENTIONS
12 CAPACITIES
12 GIFTS

BOOK THREE
YOUR SOUL'S
12 IMPRESSIONS OF I
12 ENCOUNTERS WITH THOU
12 HOMES
12 ACTS OF KINDNESS

THE ART AND PRACTICE OF INNER CHRISTMAS
THE SIX CELEBRATIONS
THE GUIDE TO THE HOLY NIGHTS

FOR MY GRANDCHILDREN
EDON, FLORA, JULIEN, SABINE
AND AVA

MAY *every day* BE CHRISTMAS.

Contents

Note From Lynn
17

Written During the Holy Nights
18

How to Unwrap the 4 Gifts of Each Message
30

Your Spiritual Companion
39

The Twelve Perceptions of Your Soul
45

Touch
49
Well-Being
51
Self-Movement
53
Balance
55
Smell
57
Taste
59
Vision
62
Warmth
64
Hearing
66
Word
68
Thought
71
Ego
74

The Twelve Prepositions of Your Soul
79

In
83

Out Of
85

Toward
87

On
89

With
91

Because Of
94

Between
97

Of
99

Through
102

Over
104

Against
106

Among
108

The Twelve Qualities of Your Soul
111

Receptivity
115

Generosity
120

Humility
124

Nobility
127

Solidity
130

Fluidity
133

Luminosity
135

Reflectivity
138

Equanimity
143

Fecundity
147

Sagacity
150

Unity
154

The Twelve Polarities of Your Soul
159

Solitude & Intimacy
163

Desire & Fulfillment
166

Movement & Stillness
170

Vertical & Horizontal
176

Freedom & Lawfulness
182

Warming & Cooling
187

Reflection & Anticipation
193

Gathering & Spreading
197

Asleep & Awake
202

Leading & Following
207

Passion & Compassion
212

Certainty & Doubt
217

Subscribe
225

My Note of Gratitude
227

About the Author Lynn Jericho
231

The Imagine Self Academy
232

Note from Lynn

Written During the Holy Nights

Of all the nights in the year, the Holy Nights are the most holy. The connection between spiritual beings and human beings is most intimate, fluid and active.

Each of the "messages" in this book was written during the Holy Nights, the twelve nights between Nativity, December 25 and Epiphany, January 6.

Why does this matter?

The Holy Nights — What makes them holy?

If you look up the definition, synonyms and root of "holy" you will find references to God, religious doctrine, sacred, wholeness, reverence and more.

For me, "holy" indicates the active presence of spiritual beings whose purpose is to design and ignite in human beings moral qualities such as truth, beauty, goodness, love, freedom, forgiveness, compassion, wisdom, wonder, awe, humor and joy.

MY PERCEPTION OF THE HOLY NIGHTS

(What I share here is both archetypal and personal. I have sought the wisdom of the Inner Year in the great teachings of humanity, but the meaning I have found came from my own efforts at deepening my experience. I urge you to do the same).

When I first heard of the Holy Nights, I had a soul feeling and a gut response that they were a spiritual reality. I thought of them as a more meaningful yearly experience than my traditional Christmas one. It was years before I realized they were the pinnacle of the Inner Year.

What is the Inner Year? A year in nature is a repetitive rhythm in time and reveals the movement and relationship between the

Sun and the Earth. Inwardly, we see it in the patterns of the moods and interests of our souls.

The human soul is a dance between spirit and matter. Throughout the (inner) year and during each (inner) day/night, our souls move back and forth between our earthly experiences and our spiritual ones. Most of the year we are hardly aware of the dance. It seems hidden by the veils of our senses and dulled by the distracting static of ordinary attitudes. The Holy Nights offer us time to dance into the spiritual realities most gracefully, wonderfully and wisely. In grace, we can wonder and be blessed with new wisdom.

The Inner Year begins with Epiphany (January 6th) and ends on Christmas Eve (December 24). Between the ending of the old Inner Year and the beginning of the new Inner Year are the mysterious twelve Holy Nights. They begin with Nativity, December 25, and end with the 5th of January, the night before Epiphany.

In most of the populated world, these nights are the darkest, coldest, most silent and most still of the natural year. But for the Inner Year they are the time of great spiritual light, great cosmic warmth, universal harmonies and dynamic inner activity. Do you feel this?

For twelve nights in time the veils lift and the signals strengthen between the spiritual world and the earthly world, between the cosmos and the individual, between your selfhood and your story. Time becomes timeless. Holiness magnifies.

Over these nights of grace, whispers and glimmers of the wonder and wisdom offer inspiration of new clarity, warmth, harmony, and design for living. The Holy Nights provide a restorative and empowering schooling for our souls. I might even say they are a "sacred spa" with profound curative properties: healing, liberating and empowering who you are and who you are becoming.

(There is much more about the design of the rest of the Inner Year on my website: imagineself.com)

We cannot benefit from the Holy Nights if we only experience them with a vague, blurry, romantic, oceanic feeling. For many years that's what I did. It was not fulfilling, supportive or transformative. I did not find it beneficial to read a holy book during the Holy Nights. Nor did I find it useful to work with the dreams I had during the Holy Nights as predictive of the coming year. Nor did a sense that the placement of the stars and the planets offered a picture of a sacred design for next twelve months. All of these ways of understanding and working with the unique experience of the Holy Nights can be truly meaningful, but I sought a path to the wisdom of the Self, a path of moral development and spiritual renewal.

Only when I began to enter the Holy Nights with a specific theme to wonder about and explore in twelve different ways in a personal, truly intimate relationship did I come to know the mystery and gifts of the Holy Nights.

The Inner Christmas Messages & the Holy Nights

On December 22, 2004, I was inspired to write "reminders" during the Holy Nights and to send them out into the world, my small mailing list of less than 200 people.

On December 23, 2004, somewhat stunned by my intention, I realized that I could design my intention and the experience best by focusing on a theme and offering twelve insights on the theme. I was to send messages. By the time I wrote the final message, I knew I had awakened a deed in my soul...I would be offering the Inner Christmas Messages every year.

I've done this every year since. Writing the messages has become my responsibility, devotion and joy.

These yearly thematic messages bring nightly gifts between the two archetypal and universal celebrations of the wonder of Divine Birth and the wisdom of Divine Manifestation. In many traditions these inner celebrations come at the Winter Solstice in nature. In the Christian path, Christmas and Epiphany are the celebrations.

The messages I write are deeply spiritual and morally creative, yet free of any outer institutionalized Christian dogma or doctrine. They do not require belief. They can benefit everyone. They simply ask that you pay attention to how you specifically experience a universally human gesture.

(In some of the messages I refer to the archetypes from the New Testament such as the Shepherds and the Kings. As archetypes, the Shepherds represent heartfelt wonder and the Kings, the pure wisdom of the devoted intellect).

THE INSPIRATIONS FOR THE INNER CHRISTMAS MESSAGES

Inspiration breathes life into possibility and the inspiration for the Inner Christmas Messages begins usually at midsummer as a long, slow, delicate inhale. I find the question "What will the theme for the Holy Nights be?" floating in and out of my consciousness as the light darkens and days shorten.

Some years the theme appears early in the summer. Other years I wait until mid-December. Some years the gestures that will live in the messages are obvious and clear. Other years the gestures seem to appear in my consciousness the morning I write them.

Inspirations cannot be defined, organized or perfected by the intellect. An inspiration is a breath of wonder and wisdom. I have learned to trust inspiration. I have learned that wonder is the source of wisdom.

I have the commitment to write the messages but the choice of the theme and its twelve gestures or expressions always seem to be given to me. I receive and relay.

In a Nutshell...

1. The Inner Christmas themes are core elements of being human and becoming I.

2. Devoted attention to the themes makes being human and imagining self holy and sacred.

3. Working with and through 12 points of view or 12 components for each theme awakens a conscious recognition and relationship to the theme, your humanity and your individuality.

4. Each message offers insights and prompts for intimately and personally engaging with the theme.

5. The messages enhance and deepen the renewal of wonder and the development of wisdom that is possible during the Holy Nights.

every day?

The Inner Christmas messages are not just for contemplation and response during the Holy Nights. Their wonder and wisdom are there for every day of your life. They are gifts that give forever. Each message contains the active holiness of the Holy Nights.

Many times I have been asked to gather up the messages in a book or books. When I decided to do this, I needed a title. Quickly, Inner Christmas Every Day came to be.

As I reflect on these themes and messages I realize how the inspirational reality of the Holy Nights lives in the thought behind each message. Each message brings a gift from and of the Holy Nights. Work with an Inner Christmas message every day.

Each message can be taken up into your thoughts and

feelings to birth new understanding of your individuality and offer new epiphanies of wonder and wisdom. Make the theme and the gestures your own. Feel the spiritual activity in your soul. Make being you holy.

The Work of Inner Christmas Every Day

Inner Christmas is WORK. It takes effort and commitment.

It is more than the inner experience equivalent of hanging an ornament on a tree, eating a delicious desert, or a singing a beautiful carol.

If you are willing to be more than you ever thought of being, work with the messages. You will find that the moment you seek the I before, behind and beyond your ordinary experience and impressions, the whole spiritual world is at your back, applauding, encouraging and inspiring your next breath, thought, feeling and deed.

What follows are four ways to unwrap the gift in each message.

With much love,
Lynn

Note: In many of the messages I offer suggestions for working with them, questions to ask yourself and activities to engage. Some I don't. Not every theme includes an Epiphany message. Inspiration does not come with a template or a set of required tasks.

To learn more about the Holy Nights and to find inspirations for the six celebrations living in Christmas, please read "*The Art and Practice of Inner Christmas.*"

How to Unwrap the Four Gifts of Each Message

Any message any day any way. Although the title refers to every day, it is really any day you need to unwrap an inner Christmas gift.

You may want to start at the beginning of the collection and read message by message through to the 12th message of the fourth theme. You may want to keep the book of messages by your bed or at your desk and open it up to a random message because you want to feed your soul and you trust your angel to choose the right nourishment.

You may want to work with one message a day or one message a week. Or see what happens if you work with one message for four days using a different method of unwrapping each day.

Just be creative as any way any day will bring you an Inner Christmas gift.

Each message is archetypal which means each message is universal and can be unwrapped by every human soul. Yet, for every soul the message will have a unique meaning, interpretation and impact. Another mystery of the messages appears in every reading. Each reading brings a different inner experience.

Each message can offer your four gifts or more, depending on how you want to work with it...or rather unwrap it. Here is a description of each of the four gifts and the way to unwrap each one.

Find joy in each gift.

Unwrap the Gift of Brief Meditations

The INNER CHRISTMAS *every day* messages are brief meditations that encourage depth, more than length, of attention.

Though brief, the Inner Christmas meditations are neither simple nor sentimental.

They are, in fact, quite challenging and objective. Our thoughts, reflections and attention to the messages need to

go into the depths of our living,

up to the heights of our striving and

far into the wide expanse of

our manifold relationships.

Composed during the Twelve Holy Nights the messages go beyond our ordinary meditative boundaries. In reading them, you will find special gifts for spiritual, moral, and personal development and renewal.

Let me suggest this meditative process. Before you read, connect with your body and your senses. Notice any bodily tensions or discomforts and any sensory distractions. Just notice, don't stress. Relax. We live in challenging times. It's okay to be tense, uncomfortable and distracted. Now take some deep breaths and focus and extend the exhale. Smile.

Now read the message. Let the message flow into your soul. Don't think about it. Let it wrap around your heart and sing a celebration to your individuality. Be passive and open.

After the meditative reading, be still for a while. Then begin to breathe into reflections and inspirations. Quietly journal.

UNWRAP THE GIFT OF NEW CAPACITIES TO PERCEIVE YOURSELF & OTHERS

"Every object, well-contemplated, creates an organ of perception in us."
— Goethe

This quote from Goethe inspires the soul to contemplate itself. The most significant and essential organ of perception *is the organ of self-contemplation. Self-contemplation* strengthens the higher self and its capacity for freedom and love.

Each INNER CHRISTMAS *every day* theme gives you twelve ways to *contemplate* it with the messages. Each theme offers a lens for seeing yourself and for being more fully human. You have opportunity to *contemplate* your inner life using four themes each from twelve different experiences. Your *contemplations* will create your soul's organ of *self-contemplation*. You will be able to perceive and begin to understand the mystery and creativity of your soul and every other soul.

I invite you to contemplate each message:

- Read the message with innocence, not with intellect. Breathe them in and warm them up with your own sweet energy.

- In the message, you may find a thought, a phrase, a metaphor or a question that brings a burst of intrigue, confusion, or energy to your soul. Grab it! Underline or highlight it. Write it down in your journal.

- Bring it to the space of your consciousness. Imagine your consciousness as an inner space. Wherever the boundaries of your thoughts are stretched with new feelings of beautiful possibilities and your will motivates creative inner activity, this is the place to take the message, or the phrase, or the question or a word for contemplation and celebration.

Unwrap the Gift of New Insights & Questions

Think about the message as you experience it in your life. Look at your stories, your prejudices, and your assumptions. Perhaps you have never thought about the topic before. Relax and engage with openness. Attend to the wisdom as if you were going to be dependent on it for your life. This is how you make the message personal.

Create an artistic image of your experience in words, colors, forms, sounds, or movements. This might be challenging for you. It is for me, but when I do this creative contemplation, I find something in me expands, breathes, smiles and rejoices. I find intimacy with the message and the artistic experience offers insights.

The messages often include questions to consider. In working with artistic approaches to a message, you will find questions, wonderful living questions forming in your soul. Imagine the questions inviting your thoughts and feelings to dance with them to the music of possibility, self-awareness and wonder.

Unwrap the Gift of Inspiration for Sacred Conversations

Share your thoughts and feelings about the message with another person in a sacred conversation…one that nurtures and nourishes you both. Through the conversations you will find practical, moral and spiritual intimacies emerging between you and others.

With your family or a group that gathers regularly, have conversations and presentations on the theme, a message, or a phrase. Imagine Sunday brunch with the family as Inner Christmas Brunch. Create an Inner Christmas Every Week Group and meet for tea or wine and open up the gift of the message and have everyone share their thoughts and feelings. Bring it to life!

Each message brings many gifts.
Keep unwrapping them.
Make every day an Inner Christmas

Your Spiritual Companion

What makes the Holy Nights holy is the "lifting of the veils." Veils separate and obscure. For the twelve nights between Nativity and Epiphany, the veils that separate earthly existence from the realms of spirit *lift* and spiritual light allows us to see with inspired clarity.

This spiritual light would blind us to our earthly life if we did not have moral questions. Moral questions are like polarizing sunglasses that reduce the glare of sunlight. They filter light so that we can see and distinguish. The Inner Christmas messages provide themes, perspectives, metaphors, and possibilities for the moral questioning that brings the capacities for new vision and creative discernment while standing in spiritual light.

In 2014 as I prepared for the Holy Nights, I kept asking myself how we can enliven the holiness of the Holy Nights. After ten years of Inner Christmas messages, I felt something more was needed. When I realized what this new imagination was, I was delighted!

We need a spiritual companion. A spiritual comforter and challenger. A being that will keep us moving.

Who will your spiritual companion be? You get to choose! Your companion is not a fantasy. You will be surprised by the questions asked and comments offered by your spiritual companion. Just listen with your heart. You will find her/his/its presence offering humor, irony, intensity and depth to your inner life.

I have some suggestions for you to consider as you contemplate who to invite as your companion. Or maybe your companion is not one you choose, but one that you need to recognize. Be willing to be surprised.

Perhaps your angel…

As you reflect on each message during the Holy Nights, imagine inviting your angel into your consciousness so you can describe to the spiritual being your sense of the message's beauty and meaning. Talk to your angel about how this message relates to your karma and your destiny.

Remember your angel has profound and compassionate interest in how you feel about each message. Does each message have meaning for you? How does each message support your becoming you?

Perhaps a great spiritual being...

Yes. You are worthy of this powerful attention!

Buddha, Christ, or Sophia?

Maybe one of the archangels, Michael, Raphael, Gabriel, or Uriel?

Maybe a Greek, Hindu, Persian, or Egyptian deity?

A saint or an initiate...

such as Meister Eckhart, St. Teresa, Moses, St.Paul, Rudolf Steiner, Martin Luther King Jr., Mary Magdalene, Shakespeare, Zarathustra. There are so many!

A relative beyond the threshold of time and space...

You might also share the message with your no-longer living great-grandparents or your unborn great-grandchildren. You inherited parts of of yourself from your ancestors and you will be leaving aspects of yourself to your descendants. Ancestors would ask you different questions about how you understand each message from those your descendants would ask.

You may find it difficult to pick just one companion. Let one pick you!

After reading the Inner Christmas message, ask your spiritual companion to give you a question. Write it down. You may find there are several questions. If you take the questions to heart, you will learn so much about yourself. Not only are the veils that separate you from the spiritual world lifting, but working with your companion means you are lifting the veils of control. Imagine the mood of the threshold, where and when all appearances fade and you see yourself in compassionate freedom...the way your spiritual companion sees you.

44

The
Twelve Perceptions
of Your Soul

The Gifts of Perceiving

46

These twelve messages illuminate how we perceive
- our inner experience,
- what lives outside of us, and
- all that lives in another's soul.

Essentially, we come to understand how ordinary sense experiences can reveal so much about the life of our souls.

The more we understand these twelve perceptions the more we will discover the gifts of perceiving. Perception becomes acute with wonder. We experience nuance, detail and connection. Life becomes richer.

To perceive what lives inside our skins and inside our souls we need the four senses of embodiment:
TOUCH, WELL-BEING, MOVEMENT, AND BALANCE.

To perceive what lives beyond the boundary of our skin and our sense of self, we need the four senses of earthly participation:

SMELL, TASTE, VISION, AND WARMTH.

To perceive what lives within the skin and soul of another human being we need the four senses of love:

HEARING, WORD, THOUGHT AND EGO.

These messages were written during the Holy Nights 2004/05.

THE THEME 2004/05

The Soul's First Perception
Touch

Imagine your beginning. Not necessarily your conception or your birth, but the heart of who you are and why you are here today in this moment.

Look inside your skin to find this beginning - that's where your heart's beginning lives. (We will begin looking outside our skin in a few days.) Try to touch the holiest part of your soul. This is the part of you that is always innocent, never feels lonely and has so much light and warmth that it is like a small sun inside of you.

Think of touching base, touching home plate. What are the bases you want to touch in your soul? When you touch them what do you perceive? Is your heart your home plate? How do you know you have touched it?

When we touch something in the world we meet resistance.

Whatever we touch pushes us back into ourselves. We experience NOT self. When we touch something in our soul, we experience SELF. We are embraced with the fulness of self.

This is an imagination, not a test. Just spend a few moments touching something in your soul before you go to sleep tonight

THE FIRST HOLY NIGHT 2004

The Soul's Second Perception
WELL-BEING

With the first perception we touched the light in our souls. With the second perception, we will visit the shadows.

Consider the well-being of your soul. Well-being is the absence of "the sins of the world" in body and soul. What is significant about well-being is that when "all is well" we do not notice it; we are just in the blessed moment. We attend to well-being only when it is not wholly present. For a few minutes be still and sense the presence of your well-being. Seek the glad tidings in your soul.

Then let the parts of your soul's inner being where you find hunger, thirst, weariness or pain, begin to speak of your needs for nourishment, quenching, rest and healing. Write these needs down in your holy heart center (and on paper if you wish.) Make a list of your needs as if they were your Christmas list.

The desired gifts of your list will not be found under a tree and they are never discounted. They will appear in the metamorphosing of your thoughts, feelings and deeds during your life.

It is in this experience of well-being that you can uncover the giving and receiving in your soul between your own individual kernel of the Divine and the earthly karma of your lifetime.

THE SECOND HOLY NIGHT 2004

The Soul's Third Perception
Self-Movement

Now sense your inner movement - the ease of your journey toward your goals. This is the reflection of your path of growth and development. There is a dance of development in every area of your life and soul. The earth and the planets and the stars are never still and always sensitive to each other.

Likewise, the constant movements in your soul life are mutually sensitive to the movements in your daily life of work and relationships. Are your goals and your activity in alignment? Do the demands of your life trip up your desires or do you skip along merrily?

Are you moving with more ease tonight than last night or last year? What new moves do you want to develop tomorrow and over the course of the coming year?

Where is your inner movement graceful or awkward? Do you

resist soul movement wanting only to remain the same or do you rush eagerly through new poses, new leaps, new reaches to become something your feel you must become?

THE THIRD HOLY NIGHT 2004

The Soul's Fourth Perception
Balance

This fourth perception is last one that will be reminding you of the experiences you have that focus on your sense of self within yourself. The fifth through eighth perceptions will take us into the world of nature.

There is a wonderful Latin word that has special significance during these reflections — fulcrum. Fulcrum is the point of purchase that allows for the support of a revolving object. It is the core experience of balance in your soul and on it all the activity of your inner life orients itself.

This perception of balance strengthens your fulcrum. Your inner life is the abiding fulcrum of your daily existence.

Consider the balance of your life. Find one or two polarities like thinking and willing, giving and receiving, joy and suffering or speaking and listening. Which end of the pole are you closer to?

Does this create a sense of harmony for you? If you tend toward one side, why? How does this effectively support the real goals of your life?

THE FOURTH HOLY NIGHT 2004

The Soul's Fifth Perception
Smell

Our soul's perceptions bring us into a greater intimacy with both Nature and Spirit. If we attend to our whole inner life we can almost smell the sacred aromas of both worlds. These aromas awaken and heal our souls.

The sense of smell is the sense that cannot resist or defend as it is so linked to life giving and sustaining respiration. A smell goes right into your soul.

Imagine the spirit world breathing you in as if you were giving it life. What scent would you offer?

And Nature…how does she know your odor? Do you make her glad at your presence in her varied world? Do you remind her of winter, spring, summer or fall?

Are your thoughts, feelings and deeds like a baby's breath or lily of the valley or a pine forest, or fresh-fallen snow?

Contemplating your self in metaphors can surprise you with new self-knowledge. They can give you imaginations of your intimate relationship to spirit and nature.

INHALE DEEPLY, EXHALE GENTLY

THE FIFTH HOLY NIGHT 2004

The Soul's Sixth Perception
Taste

As we consider our relationship to Nature and Spirit let's work with the metaphor of the four tastes - sweet, sour, salty and bitter. We only taste those things that we choose to take into our bodies or, in this case, into our souls.

Each taste gives our soul a certain feeling:

- *Sweet tastes give us an immediate sense of being special and good.*

- *Sour tastes wake us up and get our juices flowing.*

- *Salty tastes enhance and intensify our attention.*

- *Bitter tastes chase desire away and indicate a purification or healing property.*

Reflect over the last year. What have you tasted of Nature and

Spirit that has given your soul these feelings?

In the coming year if Nature is to taste your deeds and Spirit is to taste your thoughts, what in you will they savor?

Here is a verse by Rudolf Steiner.
Imagine Life's fruits, as Life's tastes.

The soul's questings are quickening.
The will's deeds are waxing.
And Life's fruits grow ripe.
I feel my destiny. My destiny finds me.
I feel my star. My star finds me.
I feel my goals. My goals find me.
My soul and the world are but one.
Life becomes brighter about me.
Life becomes harder for me.
Life becomes richer within me.

The last three lines of this verse could be rewritten to reflect the four tastes. Is the bright life sweeter? Saltier? Is the hard life more sour? More bitter? Is the rich life a life ready to taste everything?

Certainly the experience of the soul and the world being one involves the process of taste and leads to digestion. I taste the world. The world tastes my soul. We digest each other. We are one.

THE SIXTH HOLY NIGHT 2004

The Soul's Seventh Perception
VISION

Imagine how we see and how we are seen.

A dear friend once asked me to meditate on two possible gestures behind my deeds in the world. He wondered if my inner experience was "See me." Or "I see." The first is a needy gesture and the second a gesture of generosity. Most of us need to be seen before we can see.

How do you need or want to be seen by others? Is it your thoughts, your feelings or your deeds that long for recognition?

Are there things you see, that you are longing to share with others? If you did not worry about how you would be seen, would you be free to give your vision to others? Here are two stanzas from a verse given by Rudolf Steiner to adolescents. We have a lot to see.

I look into the world
In which the sun is shining.
In which the stars are sparkling.
In which the stones repose;
Where living plants are growing,
Where sentient beasts are living,
Where man, soul-gifted, gives
The spirit a dwelling place.
I look into the soul
That lives within my being.
The World-Creator moves
In sunlight and in soul-light
In wide world space without,
In soul-depths here within.

THE SEVENTH HOLY NIGHT 2004

The Soul's Eighth Perception
Warmth

Let's attend to the perception of warmth. Through warmth we are permeated with the quality of something beyond our skin. Unlike smell, taste or sight with which we actively take in the world, warmth moves into us without our activity.

We say something is "heartwarming" and we can feel "chilled to the bone." Warmth comes from without but is perceived deep within us.

Bring your thoughts to the warming of your soul. What do you see outside yourself that warms your inner being? And what in this world turns you cold?

With the chilling experiences, how could you warm them? Redeeming the cold with your inner warmth, radiating your strength of spirit into the shadows of our world, is a great challenge these days.

A woman was walking to a concert in NYC on a cold, bitter night and was approached by a homeless person asking for money. She gave him some coins and looked him in the eye. "What is your name?" she asked. He looked at her and answered "Daniel. No one has asked me my name in years."

How do you warm chilled hearts?

THE EIGHTH HOLY NIGHT 2004/05

The Soul's Ninth Perception
HEARING

The first four perceptions we explored the experiences of being in ourselves, contained within the boundary of our skin. The middle four nights we looked at how we experience the world outside our skin. With the closing four we will be working with our perceptions of what lives within other human beings.

Consider the voice and tone of those close to you. What resounds in your soul when you contemplate a loved one or friend? When you listen to the voice of another your soul is resonating to their soul. This is the perception of hearing.

Our ears are shaped like question marks. When we hear another, we ask in our soul questions about the individual speaking and find answers in attending to the echoes of their being that resonate within our being. To do this we must be truly silent and still.

In the stillness and silence of your soul, recall a conversation you had during the day. Forget the words. Focus on the voice, breath and tone of the other. What do you hear?

There is a wonderful Irving Berlin song with the lyric "The song is ended, but the melody lingers on."

Listen to what lingers on in your soul.

With listening we move from warmth to a deeper, more crystallized experience in our soul.

When as the voice of love
Man gives himself as soul unto the world,
When through resounding tone
Man echoes the spirit of the world,
Then in spirit-chiming soul,
Then in soul-singing spirit,
Will spirit man in earthly man
Be truly heard.

THE NINTH HOLY NIGHT 2004/05

The Soul's Tenth Perception
WORD

This is the tenth perception and the second one that we attend to how we know others. Each contemplation will require more awareness. Yesterday we listened for the music in another's voice. Tonight we will experience their language.

Each of us has our own idiosyncratic language. These are the little phrases that we unconsciously and thoughtlessly insert into or tack on to our statements, questions, comments, etc. Because they are spoken so frequently, they seem meaningless, but they reveal so much about us. It is our constant refrain.

Some examples:

> *Listen to this!*
>
> *But that's okay.*
>
> *Think about it.*

As a matter of fact.

Gothcha!

You won't believe this.

If you will.

Because there is no thought behind these phrases, we tend to ignore them or find them irritating. Yet if we were to give an impersonation of a person, these phrases of theirs would be essential. We need to understand why this phrase has become so much a part of their language.

Choose someone you are very close to and recall one of his or her idiosyncratic phrases. What do you learn about this person if you reflect on the significance and meaning of this thoughtless phrase? This task of reflection is not about analyzing the speaker; rather it is about feeling their hidden personality revealed in their oft-repeated words.

At Christmas, I love to grow amaryllis in my home. I know so well their idiosyncratic way of growing and unfolding their blooms. I realize with this language exercise that I am remembering what I already know about all amaryllis rather than seeing this particular flower. Because memory is so easy, I remember rather than perceive.

Forget your memories, now is the time to heighten and strengthen our abilities to perceive anew.

THE TENTH HOLY NIGHT 2004/05

The Soul's Eleventh Perception
Thought

In the tenth perception, we developed a feeling for another by attending to their "thoughtless" words. For the eleventh perception we will reverse the process and seek to know how they uniquely express a universal or archetypal thought in their own individual words and actions.

This is a lovely exercise as it takes us into both the soul of the individual and the soul of the Cosmos. There is a cosmic realm of thoughts that we all can access with our thinking. We share this vast store of universally known ideas and ideals but what makes us individual and unique is the way each of us interprets, evolves and expresses them. We each take responsibility to create relationship with a universally shared concept in our own way.

Bring into your heart a universal concept such as love, freedom, courage, trust, longing, fulfillment, wonder, etc. Then bring into your heart someone you know well. Ask yourself how this individual uniquely expresses the ideal you have chosen.

Challenge yourself to recall the spoken words and evident deeds that reveal this individual's particular relationship to this concept. Do not be influenced by how much sympathy or antipathy you bear for this person. Do your best to be objectively observant.

Through this contemplation you will find in yourself a growing capacity to know others and to find more awareness of how these ideals from this cosmic realm of thoughts enter into the human soul and into our earthly interactions.

Here is a verse from Rudolf Steiner that speaks to the flowing rhythm between the cosmos and the individual.

Seek in your own being

And you will find the world;

Seek in worldwide being

And you will find yourself;

Note the constant swing

Between self and world

THE ELEVENTH HOLY NIGHT 2004/05

The Soul's Twelfth Perception
Ego

We began with the first perception seeking to touch the "holy of holies," the pure spirit of our own individuality. With the twelfth perception, we seek to be aware of that spirit in another human being.

The reflections on perceiving the other, not as a visible physical being but as being of soul and spirit, demand that we move from a materialistic sensitivity to a spiritual sensitivity. How do we awaken the spiritual in our souls so that we can sense the spiritual in other human beings? How do we lift the veils that hide us from one another?

This is not easy. Perhaps success is simply the heartfelt attempt.

Begin with imagining the disappearance of the physical body of the other. Then shut out any awareness of this person's energies, biology and personal history. Move past their personal thoughts, feelings and intentions, like the prince tearing through the brambles to reach Briar Rose, the Sleeping Beauty. Finally, you find your "I" meeting the "I" of the other - both of you unclothed, pure and free.

Having achieved this meeting, you move back away, allowing the layers of karma and material existence to again clothe the kernel of the Divine you just met. But now the radiant "I Am" illuminates all your other perceptions of this individual.

You will begin to experience the fullness of your own humanity in knowing the full humanity of the other.

The perceptions have come full circle.

Here is a quote from Rudolf Steiner that encourages your work tonight.

'Create for yourself a new, indomitable perception of faithfulness. What is usually called faithfulness passes so quickly. Let this be

your faithfulness.

You will experience moments - fleeting moments - with the other person. The human being will appear to you then as if filled, irradiated with the archetype of his spirit.

And then there may be, indeed will be, other moments, long periods of time, when human beings are darkened. But you will learn to say to yourself at such times: "The Spirit makes me strong. I remember the archetype. I saw it once. No illusion, no deception shall rob me of it." Always struggle for the image that you saw. This struggle is faithfulness. Striving thus for faithfulness, we shall be close, one to another, as if endowed with the protective powers of angels.'

THE TWELFTH HOLY NIGHT 2004/05

77

78

The
Twelve Prepositions
of Your Soul

The Gifts of Relating

80

In the Twelve Prepositions we will open the gifts of relating.

Relationship is the core purpose of human consciousness. We are always in relationship: subject to object and object to subject. As subject, I am always relating to all that I know. As object, everything is always relating to me.

In all languages there are a number of tiny words that indicate the design of our relationships. These are the prepositions that define the direction and location of the subject to the object.

You can find a great list of prepositions on www.wikipedia.com if you want to continue this exploring your relationships.

One of my readers shared the following story:

"30 years ago, when I was in the US Army and attended the Defense Language School in Monterey, CA (where I learned to

speak German), I remember a teacher there, a European national who spoke a dozen languages fluently.

When someone asked him the quickest way to learn to speak a new foreign language, he gave his own experience: "I start by learning all the prepositions. They are the relationship words that bind all the other words, nouns, adjectives, even verbs together. Once I learn the prepositions, the other words attach themselves like paper clips to a magnet."

Each message will give you a preposition to wonder about and will shine new light on how you relate to all things, beginning with yourself.

These messages were written during the Holy Nights 2005/06.

THE THEME 2005/06

Your Soul's First Preposition
IN

Let's begin with *IN*.

IN represents location. The soul with its infinite activities of thoughts, feelings and intentions can find itself *in* many locations. I want to suggest four locations that feel most reflective of the First Holy Night and the experience of the Nativity of the Divine Child

Which of your thoughts, feelings or intentions are...

- *In the womb...*

...what unborn gift of your soul is developing?

- *In the tomb...*

...what soul work have you completed and laid to rest this year?

- *In process...*

...what are you actively and joyfully manifesting in your life?

- *In crisis...*

...what is stuck or rushed or unformed and needs help or guidance?

Blessings on your Incarnation.

THE FIRST HOLY NIGHT 2005

Your Soul's Second Preposition
Out Of

OUT OF is a wonderful gift to contemplate. (There are a number of two and three word prepositions like *out of* and in spite of that describe our relationship to all things.)

As human beings we have this great gift of free thinking. Our thinking can be free of the laws and necessities of our physical survival, pleasure and pain. This is the result of our uprightness and the fact that our head and spine relate at a ninety degree angle to the surface of the earth unlike animals. Our head sits above and our torso and limbs live below. Even the higher primates have pelvises that tilt them away from the heavens and toward the earth leaving them locked into the earthly demands of their lower bodies.

This gift of freedom is not without its challenge. With our heads living in the clouds above us and our bodies responding to the ground below us, we have a dual existence: one heavenly and one earthly. Our souls struggle to keep both relationships in productive harmony. This leads to our thoughts/questions for tonight.

Are you more comfortable living in your thoughts or fantasies? Do you spend most of your time *out of* your body?

Or do you prefer being *out of* your mind? I am not asking you if you are crazy, although that may be a question you have. Rather, do you do things *out of* habit or impulsivity with little consciousness? Some of us just do not like to think about things.

What parts of your life are *out of sync* with your intentions or your community?

Maybe you are a creative radical or an imaginative visionary and march, like Thoreau, to a different drummer. That drummer may be your personal spirit urging you to step *out of* line.

How do you feel about experiencing something so different it is *out of* this world and *out of* the ordinary?

May you find a great blessing that comes from *out of* the blue

THE SECOND HOLY NIGHT 2005

Your Soul's Third Preposition
TOWARD

Let's consider how *TOWARD shapes our life*.

Toward relates us to our future and to the movement in our souls.

What are you moving t*oward*? How many different places or achievements are you heading for?

Is it your thinking that is active, striving for a different way of perceiving some aspect of yourself or of the world?

Do you seek new feelings? Do you want to let go of doubts or resentments? Do you have desires that cause you suffering?

What deeds are you driving *toward*?

Many of us are bogged down with To Do lists. What we really need is a *TOWARD* list. To Do's can keep us from our *Towards.*

What gets in your way as you move *toward* your goals?

How do you help others move *toward* their dreams?

Your higher self stands on the horizon of your life and calls you *toward* your destiny.

Journey well.

P.S. Make a sign with *TOWARD* in bold letters. I am going to tape it to my bathroom mirror. It will be a great reminder

THE THIRD HOLY NIGHT 2005

Your Soul's Fourth Preposition
On

Contemplate ON.

I am depending on you to think about this little word, unless something else is on your mind. I could go on and on about the images I base my soul life on but I am going to meet a client and I must be on time and these messages are really meant to turn you on to your own soul life, not mine.

What does the health of your inner life depend on? What do you need to maintain contact with to feel supported, alive, understood?

Are there things that are always on your mind? Can you keep your focus on the things that enrich your life?

How long can you sustain a mood of peace and goodwill? Will it go on indefinitely throughout the year?

What are the foundations you stand on that give you confidence in yourself?

What is your relationship to time? Does your life flow in an organized and manageable rhythm making it easy for you to be on time?

Most importantly, what about your inner life truly turns you on?

May you stay on the bright side of life and joyfully fulfill your destiny.

THE FOURTH HOLY NIGHT 2005

Your Soul's Fifth Preposition
WITH

Please work *with* each question.

What is intended is that you become more aware of how these little words carry so much significance. Prepositions describe the ways we relate, how we are arranged, and what our circumstances and conditions are.

Each of the twelve messages support you *with* developing an imagination, a heart feeling, for the inner meaning of each preposition. Do you have a growing feeling of toward-ness, in-ness or on-ness?

Let each little word sink into your soul and rise up into your consciousness.

WITH is the preposition for tonight.

With indicates companionship, condition or attribute.

Who do you share your thoughts and feelings *with*? *With* means we are not alone. "I am with you, my friend!" indicates empathic companionship. Is it easy for you to be *with* someone? Is the circle drawn by your willingness to be *with* others large or small?

Can you be *with* new ideas or feelings easily? Do you feel more comfortable being surrounded *with* familiar thoughts and feelings? Are you obsessed *with* any thoughts or behaviors?

When we do something with someone, even if he/she is a stranger, we form a brief or enduring intimacy. The intimacy may be just physical, as for those who commute on New York City subways, or it might be spiritual, as for those who are in meditation groups. A pregnant woman is *with* child. Marriage is a commitment to share your life *with* another. We are always *with* ourselves or *with* others.

How do you do things: *with* gusto? with trepidation? *with* style? *with* love? *with* resentment? *with* courage? This *with* is like a mirror reflecting the soul moods that accompany your thoughts, feelings and actions.

Do you think *with* truth? Feel *with* beauty? Will *with* goodness?

May your heart and soul be filled *with* love.

THE FIFTH HOLY NIGHT 2005

Your Soul's Sixth Preposition
BECAUSE OF

Now we look at the preposition that addresses both the past and the future, BECAUSE OF.

Because of indicates the source or the purpose of our thoughts, feelings or actions. It is the preposition that declares "why."

Tonight you may want to look at a thought you have about yourself. You have that thought *because of* something in the past or something in the future. It is the same for your feelings and your deeds.

Whatever words follow '*because of*' reveal elements of our karma and our destiny.

If we reflect on enough of them we will see patterns and themes. The threads of our inner lives will begin to weave past and future together. Clarity often comes if we weave in both directions: from past to future and future to past. Here is an example:

In 2001, my son wanted to move out of his dorm in Manhattan. He found a sublet in an artist loft in Jersey City. *Because of* his move, I drove to Jersey City and fell in love with the energy of the city and its views of Manhattan. I moved there on July 3, 2001, into a brownstone with a view of the World Trade Towers.

I saw the Towers fall on 9/11. *Because of* my traumatic childhood I had done a great deal of inner healing work and felt a deep creative need to work with the traumatic impact of 9/11 on the individual soul. *Because of* my study of anthroposophy which came about *because of* the Waldorf school my children attended, I had a developmental picture of the human being and an understanding of the soul that became the foundation for GROUND ZERO AND THE HUMAN SOUL, the audiobook I created with my conversation partner, Bethene LeMahieu.

If I look at this story in reverse I can see that *because of* my destiny to bring this picture of the role of the individual soul in shaping the post 9/11 future, all the other *because of* events in my life needed to occur.

Besides the destiny deeds, there are all the feelings and perceptions we hold *because of* our relationships with others.

How was your soul shaped by your relationships and how does the shape of your soul shape others?

Because of is a profoundly powerful preposition.

Work with it courageously.

Always seek the source and the purpose.

THE SIXTH HOLY NIGHT 2005

Your Soul's Seventh Preposition
BETWEEN

Old and new come together for a moment at the midnight hour. And for a moment we are *BETWEEN* the two.

As a preposition *between* always has two or more objects. *Between* often means we are making a choice or finding a balance or contained within boundaries.

Our souls are the bridge *between* the spiritual and the material. Your selfhood is most at home in your humanity when you find both in dynamic balance in your daily living. This is our most sacred experience of *between*.

When the soul must make a choice *between* two or more ideas, feelings or actions, we can often find ourselves in real dilemma. It can be very helpful to imagine the results of each choice and look for the truth, beauty and goodness of each one.

This usually will take you beyond the state of dilemma and the judgment that choosing *between* a right and a wrong.

Sometimes we feel we must make a choice but what is truly best is finding a balance. I struggle with this around self-denial and self-indulgence. The balance is self-discipline, which means sometimes yes, and sometimes no, without guilt or resentment. I always felt self-discipline was the denial of desires and self-indulgence was weakness and desperation. If I had only had living in my soul a meaningful knowledge of *between,* I would have had more trust in my choices and more balance in my self-respect.

We are always sandwiched *between* who we have been and who we are becoming, this is our soul breathing. A good breathing meditation is to cherish the moment *between* the in breath and the out breath, *between* holding on and letting go. Then revere the moment *between* the out breath and the in breath, *between* keeping out and letting in.

What are you *between* in your soul?
Relish the sweet *between*.

THE SEVENTH HOLY NIGHT 2005-06

Your Soul's Eighth Preposition
OF

OF is our mysterious little word for meditation.

What are you made *of*? What are all the different talents, weaknesses, confusions, desires, mysteries, beliefs, blessings, challenges and memories that make-up your soul?

What does your daily life consist *of*? What routines, annoyances, achievements, demands, conversations, meditations, delights and pleasures occur in the hours *of* your day?

Do you spend time asking yourself what is the purpose *of* your life, the meaning *of* your existence, the significance of your thoughts or feelings or deeds?

Do you have a sense *of* humor? Do you laugh with others? Do you have a sense of play? Do you let yourself be silly now and then?

Of gives us an understanding of substance, the whole and the parts. It also gives us a sense of belonging.

What groups and gatherings are you a member *of*? Why? What groups do you long to be a part *of*? Why? Are there groups you no longer want to be a part *of*?

Why?

May your year be a year *of* growth and fulfillment, peace and forgiveness, delight and love.

Please feel the warmth *of* my heart reaching out to you.

P.S. Many of us desire our lives to be an expression *of* spiritual activism. Last night I was going through some papers and I found this meditative verse by Rudolf Steiner. I thought it was a gift *of* loving wisdom.

I would kindle every man

Out of the Spirit of the cosmos

That he become a flame

And in the fire unfold

The being of his being.

O joy when the human flame

Springs up with living fire

Even when it is at rest.

O bitterness if the human creature

Becomes bound where it would be active.

THE EIGHTH HOLY NIGHT 2006

Your Soul's Ninth Preposition
THROUGH

THROUGH will be our eighth preposition.

Everyday when I choose the preposition, I know I am allowing the soul meaning of the word to move all through my being. It is very much like listening to a musical instrument in a room with extraordinary acoustics and feeling the sound of the instrument resonate in my bones, organs, fluids and breath. Hearing an instrument is rare for most of us, but hearing these little words is commonplace. It is the mystery of the Holy Nights that allow the commonplace to be revealed as significant.

What are the themes that run *through* your life like a river *through* the countryside? Life is rich along rivers; look for the rich deposits of inner activity to show you the themes.

Consider which emotion moves *through* your feeling life. Is it anger, sadness, fear or happiness? Each of these emotions is essential to our lives. The more consciousness we bring to our emotions, the wiser we become.

Through does more than lead us to all pervading themes or feelings; it can also indicate the ending of duration. What tasks did you get *through* last year? What would you like to get *through* this year? With flying colors, without a scratch, like a breeze?

Have you broken *through* any barriers in your inner life? How have you done that? Did you have help? Did you do this *through* determination and hard work or *through* grace and surrender?

May the gods be with you all *through* the night
and the rest of the year.

You will get *through* the thick and the thin of it all.

THE NINTH HOLY NIGHT 2005-06

Your Soul's Tenth Preposition
OVER

OVER is the little word for the tenth gift.

There are two songs from my childhood that I sang many times. They shaped my sense of life. They are *"Over the Rainbow"* and *"The Bear Went Over The Mountain."*

One song gave me hope, the other frustration and resignation.

Over The Rainbow told me there was a place over there that was better than over here. Where do you long for rainbows? If you could get *over* the rainbow what would you find? How would you be different?

No matter how many mountains the bear climbs *over*, she only finds another mountain. What in your life is an endless loop of sameness? Climbing mountains takes such effort when you can't anticipate a new vista.

Over indicates change, effort, degree and closure.

What is *over* the top in your personality or your life? Do you set goals and then work to surpass them? Do you work to limit the extremes of your behaviors, moods and needs?

When something is *over* we either celebrate or grieve, often we need to do both. Do you celebrate well? Do you grieve well? If you have trouble with either of these inner feelings, you may not allow parts of your life to be *over* even when they are *over*. What do you need to get *over*?

May you experience an *over*abundance of love.

THE TENTH HOLY NIGHT 2005-06

Your Soul's Eleventh Preposition
AGAINST

AGAINST is our eleventh preposition.

Against reveals a number of opposing relationships of varying intensities.

We can find support and comfort when we rest *against* something. It is as if there is blessing to this opposition. In our souls when we are stressed or weary and not up to a new way of thinking or feeling, we rest *against* our understood and familiar ways. What calming thoughts and inspiring meditations do you rest *against*?

Do you ever find yourself swimming *against* the tide in your thinking? Does this feel like you will drown or like you are finding your way to new shores of consciousness?

Do your ideals compete with your reality? Does your reality fight against your ideals? How can you bring them into harmony?

Our lives are often measured by how we respond when we come up *against* the challenges of living. This is true outwardly and inwardly. When you resist new inner experiences or you find limits to your inner growth, the mood of your soul is expressed in the preposition *against*. In this mood you will be either rigid or fluid? By understanding your relationship to *against* you will find more grace in moving between rigidity and fluidity.

During these Holy Nights did you brush up *against* something new in your inner life? Pay attention to it.

May your star shine brightly *against* the darkness of the night.

THE ELEVENTH HOLY NIGHT 2005-06

Your Soul's Twelfth Preposition
Among

Our twelfth little word with big meaning in our souls is **AMONG**.

Among all the ways you identify yourself:
- *as a physical body of form and health,*
- *as a participant in many conversations and activities,*
- *as a collection of points of view, emotional needs and reactions,*
- *as a set of intentions, desires and wishes,*
- *as a treasure of ideals and aspirations,*
- *as a measure of joys and sufferings,*

do you find a core, inviolable, radiant Selfhood?

Among all your reflections on prepositions did you find a growing sense of the Selfhood that is always evolving, yet always beyond alteration?

Among all the possibilities that call out to you, do you recognize your path to freedom in your thinking and love in your deeds?

Among all the reverberations ringing through your soul, do you hear the harmonies that sing I AM, I AM, I AM?

P. S. A colleague of mine shared this quote from Rudolf Steiner. I find the last line quite moving.

'Daemon-Genius is another phrase for Selfhood, Higher Self, I AM. I am going to sleep. Until awakening, my soul will be in the Spiritual World. There will it meet the guiding Being of my earthly life who abiding in the Spiritual World hovers around my head; there will it meet the Daemon-Genius. And when I awaken, I will have met the Daemon-Genius. The wings of my Daemon-Genius will have beaten upon my soul.'

THE TWELFTH HOLY NIGHT 2005-06

110

The
Twelve Qualities
of Your Soul

The Gifts of Characterizing

How these twelve qualities of soul are configured in our own souls shapes our character.

Our souls have a central core of foundational qualities that support our growth and development as we face our struggles between our own noble ideals and our base instincts and temptations. A soul quality is a feature, a characteristic, a property, a gesture, an element and a significance shaping and living in our personality. A foundational quality supports and sustains the consciousness of who we are and the unique characterization of our individuality.

All Twelve Qualities of Soul are present in each of us. Individually, we relate to the different qualities with greater or lesser levels of consciousness and expression. Some of us may struggle with awakening to luminosity, but find our sense of unity deep and profound. Our task is to work with the twelve qualities with a goal of strengthening each one. Soul qualities have a living truth, they grow and evolve over our lifetimes as long as we give them attention and give ourselves objective compassion and enthusiastic encouragement.

These messages were written during the Holy Nights 2006/07.

THE THEME 2006/07

Your Soul's First Quality
Receptivity

Look into the mood of Nativity, of birth and innocence and openness. Seek the quality of receptivity in your soul.

The innocence of the newborn is found in the total receptivity to all things earthly. The babe is newly born out of the spirit and into the earthly. There are two aspects of this earthly receptivity: need and wonder.

The infant needs to receive all that is required for survival: breastmilk, warmth, love, protection. The infant wonders at all that meets the senses: light and colors, sounds and textures, smells and tastes. As the months pass by the infant wonders at and needs the mystery of awakening thoughts and feelings and the power to move the body and to move and grasp things.

As we grow up, older and wiser our inborn earthly innocence decreases, but our need and wonder increase and evolve.

Receptivity requires more consciousness to be fulfilling.

Meeting our needs becomes complicated with demand, denial and rejection. Make a list of your needs and the challenges to remaining open in spite of denial, rejection and lack of satisfaction.

Stimulating wonder becomes a matter of willed and enthusiastic attention and interest. Our day-to-day lives are taken for granted and become ordinary if we forget to attend to the miracles hidden in the mundane. Make a list of wonder. Write down "I will attend to and wonder at..."

Language is very powerful. We commonly say "I wonder if...." which leaves us without the force of our own will. But if we change the preposition from "if" to "at", wonder becomes a meaningful, intentional deed. We become actively receptive in our souls.

Let's wonder at what we need and why we need it. Let's acknowledge how very much we need to wonder.

Our adult souls need to wonder in order to receive the new and the deep and the profound. We need to wonder at our humanity and our soulfulness.

Go into your soul and contemplate how awake or conscious you are of your receptivity to both what you need and what you could wonder at. Are you open to receiving? What do you need in your life? How many times a day do you wonder at what has come into your life?

Do you put limits on what you receive? Some souls are too receptive others are not receptive enough. What is the healthy balance of receptivity for you?

Do you seek to receive from the Spiritual World? What needs do you have that can only be met by being receptive to spirit? Can you only receive from the spirit those gifts that are defined by a religious or cultural dogma or belief system? Does your spiritual path take you on journeys into many religious and cultural landscapes. Do you allow yourself to wonder at spiritual imaginations that are unfamiliar and receive new inspirations?

Perhaps you are someone who spends the year rejecting

materialism. Could you be receptive to the gifts of matter? Perhaps you struggle with your own earthiness? Many of us can live richer lives if we are receptive to the experiences of embodiment.

When we meet what is asking to be received with prejudice and assumption we have lost all innocence. We miss the chance to grow, to be surprised, to know delight. Yet we cannot be naïve. How can we be both wise to false gifts from either spirit or matter and yet sustain the receptive openness of innocence?

Perhaps it is in being sensitive to the presence of love. Not a desire that seduces and triggers hunger, but the love that calmly awakens us and leaves us free to choose.

What gifts did you receive today or in the last year from spirit and matter? Remember it is our soul's receptivity that is the bridge between both realities.

How were you enriched by life?
By introspection? By relationships?

What do you seek to receive tomorrow or in the coming year?

Surrounding receptivity in our souls is thankfulness. Gratitude will drive out the clouds of fear and anxiety from our souls. Spend a few moments feeling the fullness of gratitude. Gratitude is the blessing of our receptivity.

THE FIRST HOLY NIGHT 2006

Your Soul's Second Quality
GENEROSITY

My heart always feels awe at this wisdom of the German poet and scientist, J. W. Goethe:

"Human Life runs its course in the metamorphosis between receiving and giving."

First we must receive. Like a newborn, the first deed is to inhale and experience our own life forces being awakened.

Then we must give. The second deed of the newborn is to exhale and announce to the world "I am here! I come to give something that only I can give!" At that moment the gift may only be breath that has been warmed by a tiny body and a yell or squeal of new life, but what a generous beginning.

What is it that you came into this life to give?
And how do you give it?

Sadly, we can give without generosity. When we are generous we give out of our true being, of our Selfhood. There is grace present in the gesture of generosity. That grace is what Goethe refers to when he speaks of the metamorphosis between receiving and giving.

What have you received in the last year that has metamorphosed into something only you can give? Can you articulate how it metamorphosed in your soul? Did you spend time thinking about it or looking at it from different perspectives? Did you find yourself embracing it with deep feeling? Did you actively begin to work with what you received until it became something new and different? These are the ways the soul makes something it has received into something it can give generously.

Yes, we can pass things on without metamorphosis. But the ability to give something you have worked with, into and through imbues the gift with your spirit. It becomes a truly generous gift.

Perhaps the dearest gift the soul can give to all things is attention. Can you meet all you perceive or imagine with true, unselfish interest?

Do you realize that spiritual beings seek your attention? How do we attend to spiritual beings? When you pray do you attend to the beings you pray to or are you only asking them to attend to you? Have you ever had a listening conversation with an angel?

Not so long ago, most human souls gave their attention to nature beings. Most of us can remember doing this in our childhoods. When I give my program on "Having Conversations with Spiritual Beings" I ask my audience if they ever interacted with a spiritual being. I am not surprised when everyone responds with an experience from childhood (when we were innocent). Most speak of talking with nature spirits. Do you remember?

The materialistically educated mind has often lost the capacity to attend generously to these nature spirits.

I found another quote about generosity of spirit. This one is by Ralph Waldo Emerson.

"There is no beautifier of complexion, or form, or behavior, like the wish to scatter joy and not pain around us. 'Tis good to give a

stranger a meal, or a night's lodging. 'Tis better to be hospitable to his good meaning and thought, and give courage to a companion. We must be as courteous to a man as we are to a picture, which we are willing to give the advantage of a good light."

Do you generously shine your good light on others?

If your good light is often hiding behind the dark clouds of disdain, envy or disinterest, consider why. Who has shone their good light on you? How did it feel?

As you go to bed tonight, imagine 3 people and generously shine your good light on each one. Can you do that every night? Imagine how filled with generosity your soul will be. Imagine how that will change your days.

The Second Holy Night 2006

Your Soul's Third Quality
Humility

Humility is often misunderstood.

Each of us is made up of a myriad of strengths and weaknesses. Each strength and each weakness creates a self-perception and a self-judgment. And these perceptions and judgments tend to distort our sense of our self-worth and self-esteem. Our thinking, feeling and willing get entangled with our strengths and weaknesses. Often our soul life ends up in a mess. Humility is the quality that begins to clear the mess.

We create the mess to hide the weaknesses. Humility allows us to honor our weaknesses. Through humility, we can be generous to ourselves and shine a good light into the dark corners of our individual humanity. We see the totality of our being and see ourselves as a whole far greater than the sum of our parts.

Humility allows us to stand strong in our own earthly (humus) being. It teaches us about our particular temperamental constitution. (The Greeks referred to the temperaments as the four humours).

Humility leads us to the core of our humanity. Sadly, so many of us think humility leads us to hate our humanity. It is only the lack of humility that makes us vulnerable to humiliation.

When something is planted in rich humus, it grows! The gift of humility is the capacity to strive towards our ideals. Our so-called weaknesses contain the greatest potential for self-esteem and inner growth.

Can you lovingly and with blessed humility make a list of your "weaknesses?" What aspects of you are hidden with denial, shame, guilt or neglect? Where in your complexity are you "less than?" Can you write down ten weaknesses?

Counting this quality, we have ten qualities remaining for contemplation. If each contemplation in the"good light" of your own self-compassion, you innocently "wonder at" one weakness from your list you will begin to see new directions and possibilities open up. Humility is the way to both self-acceptance and self-development.

Have a meditative conversation with your weakness. Ask it questions. What are you teaching me? Why are you here? What would happen to you if I embraced your presence in my life with deep humility?

I want to say, "Trust me!" but it is really about trusting yourself.

THE THIRD HOLY NIGHT 2006

Your Soul's Fourth Quality
NOBILITY

Most of us think of polarities as opposites: love is the opposite of hate; happy is the opposite of sad; rich is the opposite of poor. Our oppositional understanding keeps us at odds with ourselves. We seek one pole to avoid the other. We stay in a place of judgment without understanding.

We might find more wisdom if we looked at polarities as complements or completions of one another. This feeling is that *you can't have one without the other*. In my thoughts on the qualities of soul, I am working with the imagination of dear companions rather than struggling opponents. I want us individually to sense each quality on its own and then to see that, without the apparent opposite quality, the soul would be out of balance and have no living center. We cannot embrace one quality if we deny the essential companionship of its opposite.

What is the complement of humility? Having begun a more

conscious and loving attention to humility in our souls, we turn to its dearest companion, nobility.

Where does nobility live in your soul? Where in your soul are you nobly close to the spiritual ideals of Truth, Beauty and Goodness? If we strive to be aware of our own noble gifts and work to understand our nobility, we will become more graceful in developing (not overcoming) those aspects of soul that are challenged and uncertain.

Find your soul's nobility. What aspect of your being is so rich in talent that it declares you capable of providing superior benefit to others? Nobility of soul does not entitle you to benefits denied others. Where does your cup runneth over? Where do you offer drink to quench the thirst of other's souls?

Nobility is kindness that arises out of being special in some way. Each and every one of us is special or superior in some way. We have our own greatness. Using the quality of humility, you meditated on your weaknesses, those areas of personal existence where you lack. Each of us is less than others in some way. Observe yourself from the center of your soul and see the full spectrum of your talents.

The totality of our individuality is the complement of our humility and our nobility. It is not the denial of one by the other. Do you sometimes deny one or the other? If you are like me your answer is "Of course!" Why?

In your journal, write down your talents and abilities to perceive the world, to think ideas, to express feelings and to fulfill intentions. How do you share these talents and abilities with others?

Make a list of those individuals, living and dead, whose nobility of soul fills you with awe. Have an imaginary conversation with one of them about her nobility. Ask her questions. Listen to her answers. Be willing to be surprised by her responses.

If you struggle with allowing your nobility to express itself, ask the Spiritual World for guidance.

THE FOURTH HOLY NIGHT 2006

Your Soul's Fifth Quality
SOLIDITY

In need of a vacation do you think of heading to the mountains or heading to the beach. With this quality we are going to the mountain of the soul. With the next quality we are going to the beach.

Most of us imagine a mountain as solid. It feels as if it is made of the same material throughout. It is without any interior empty space. It feels whole and without holes.

A mountain feels ancient. It appears to have existed since the beginning.

A mountain supports us with resistance and demands that we contain ourselves. It cannot hold us, embrace us or surround us even though we cling to it and fear dropping away from it.

When we climb to the summit of a mountain, we can see far

and wide in all directions. We find ourselves at the top of the world, as if we have reached the point where the solid earth meets the airy heavens.

Seek the mountain within your soul. Find the solidity of your soul — the sense of being, of existence, that you stand on. Seek the feeling of you that is solid. Feel it in your feet. Feel it in your breath. Feel it in your thoughts. Feel it when you say I am.

The inner mountain of the soul is the part of your soul that is always in conversation with God. It is the summit of your soul. The solidity of your soul is where the inner sun is always shining.

The solidity of the soul will not crumble or fail to exist. It is the part of you that always has been and always will be. It has not gender, nor dogma, nor attitude. It is always balanced and upright.

Your soul's solidity cannot be harmed and it does not perpetrate. It resists temptation.

Simply feel your soul's solidity. Like the solidity of the planet supports your physical body, this solid core of your soul, supports your inner life.

THE FIFTH HOLY NIGHT 2006

Your Soul's Sixth Quality
FLUIDITY

Now we go from the solid certainty of our inner mountain to our inner beach where we can study the fluidity of our soul seas.

The gift of fluidity is inner gracefulness in meeting all things. Fluid has no shape of its own and yields easily to all pressure, movement and boundary.

Fluids freely shape and reshape to fit their containers and adapt to boundaries, always maintaining a perfect fit, yet the integrity of the fluid does not change.

Where solidity and the mountain resist, fluidity and the sea surrender. A fluid soul moves around with grace. It surrounds and embraces with love. It never attaches or becomes rigid.

Mountains seem forever, but moving fluids seem momentary. We can hold a solid rock in our hands but a fluid flows out, even ice is only a brief solidity. Fluids always want to return to the fluid state.

Are your thoughts too rigid? Are your feelings too frozen? Is it hard to keep your deeds freely flowing?

Fluidity as a quality of your soul, keeps your love unconditional. It nurtures freedom.

THE SIXTH HOLY NIGHT 2006

The Soul's Seventh Quality
Luminosity

Luminosity begins the second half of Your Soul's Twelve Qualities. Now that I have written "second half," I pause to think about what that means.

In our earthly world of time and space we can divide everything and consider the distance from the beginning or to the end. In pure spirit, there is not measurement. Everything is wholeness, completeness and present. Within our earthliness, we have moved through six of the qualities and have six to go. Within in our spirit, we dwell eternally in the Holy.

What in your soul is transitory and evolving? What is eternal? Again it is a good thing to write down twelve answers to each question. If you struggle to find twelve, make up some. We are not looking for correct or certain answers. We are simply looking for food for thought - a menu of soul food. In fact I want to encourage you to include in all your lists a few imaginary responses. The fruits of your imagination will always hold the sweet surprises of self-knowing.

In your list of answers we want to look for the sources of this soul quality, luminosity. Your soul's luminosity is the light that shines out from you — shining into the world and shining into the heavens.

You are luminous! You are a radiant beam of sun forces. Luminosity grows through your own capacity to evolve and your capacity to reveal the eternal within your transitory life.

Some of us have difficulty holding this awareness of luminosity. We suffer with clouds of guilt and shame. Next to your lists of the transitory and the eternal in your soul, write down the ways in which you block your inner sun with negative self-judgment.

Clouds are not fixed in nature. Nor are they fixed in your soul. They move and they disperse. And in nature the sun seems brightest when the darkest clouds move by.

In the darkest moments of your life in the last year, what

luminous aspects of your soul or of the soul of another shone forth and lit the way for you?

Look clearly into your luminous soul. Ask yourself how you will enlighten your thoughts, feelings and deeds tomorrow, over the next twelve months and for the rest of your life. How will your thoughts, feelings and deeds evolve to reveal more of what is eternal? What support do you need? What inner and outer, earthly and spiritual inspirations and resources will you seek out? What darkness will you penetrate with your own light?

THE SEVENTH HOLY NIGHT 2006/07

Your Soul's Eighth Quality
Reflectivity

The luminous quality of the soul shines out into the world. Each of us creates images in the world. Every simple thought we have, every breath we take and give, every moment of joy or sadness alters the cosmos.

With the reverse gesture the world shines into the mirrors of our souls. Every earthly perception, whether or not we have focused on it, is captured in our souls. There are infinite images and most are filed in the storage bins of unconsciousness. An ordinary mirror simply reflects back what it has been given. Our souls have a far more complex and transformative reflectivity. We want to enhance the soul quality of reflectivity.

We can develop an inner discipline that raises our earthly and spiritual powers of knowing and ensouling the world. Ensouling is the soul's reflectivity. How do you ensoul images? When we take hold of an image in our soul and give it some objective attention we penetrate and transmute the spiritual essence in the image. We polish the soul's mirror so new images are reflected back to the world bearing greater spiritual light.

With active, willed reflectivity, we can embrace all that lives in the world and imbue it with our own inner wisdom. If we meet these reflections with disdain or neglect, we endarken the images. If we meet them with loving objectivity, we add to the images the light of our higher soul forces. Then these enhanced images are reflected back to the world in a brighter way.

There is a simple exercise that can help each of us build this kind of reflectivity.

At first we can focus on harmonious images, or the ones we can consciously and comfortably contain. A bird that flew above us, two children playing together, a poem or a song, the shape of the key you use to open your door, or even a paperclip. Allow the image to enliven your thinking and write down five thoughts about the image. Now read the statements and see if you have written anything that might be considered a judgment, even a positive one. If there is judgment, cross the thought out and find another thought free of prejudice. (A prejudice is a scratch or distortion on the soul's mirror and diminishes the truth of the image being reflected) e.g. A blue ribbon is simply a blue ribbon. It is not a beautiful blue ribbon. Beautiful is a judgment.

As we grow in this practice, it becomes possible to embrace images that make us uncomfortable or ones that stimulate a wave of negative prejudices. Our negative prejudice increases and hardens the negativity of the image. When we let go of our prejudice and meet the image with a calm discernment the darkness of the image begins to soften and fade. Keep working with the five statement practice. Eventually, your soul's mirror will become incredibly clear and the most negative of images coming from the world will return to the world in a redeemed state.

If many of us develop this capacity to ensoul the images of our times, good is increased and evil diminished.

Begin by attending to one worldly image that appeared in the mirror of your soul today. Gaze into your soul's mirror with soft eyes. (Soft eyes are liquid and receiving. Hard eyes are guarded and resistant. We look at our computers and televisions with hard eyes.) If you find attending to an abstract image challenging, begin to look at a pleasing object locally and bring your awareness to your eyeballs. As you breath begin to let your eyeballs sink into your head. Instead of reaching your eyes out to the object, let the object come to your eyes. When working with a remembered object, let your inward looking eyes relax n the same way. Let the remembered image come to you.

Write down your five thoughts. Then study your thoughts. If you find you have more than five thoughts, let them go and wait a few minutes. Begin the exercise all over again. Let the next five thoughts float up from the image toward you. Write them down. You can do this as many times as you wish.

Soon the reflection of the world will be distinct and clear. Your wisdom of the world will grow. You will be actively ensouling the world.

When we do this kind of exercise, those beings in the spiritual world that live behind the mirrors of our souls can see into the world through our reflectivity. They begin helping us in this deeply human task.

THE EIGHTH HOLY NIGHT 2006/07

Your Soul's Ninth Quality
Equanimity

The Merriam-Webster dictionary defines equanimity as "calm mind." For most of us a calm soul in today's crazy, intense world is a momentary miracle. The thesaurus relates equanimity to "composure." Imagine sustaining a calm composition of soul.

Equanimity is a quality of the feeling life. If our feelings are calm and well-composed both our thoughts and our activities have a serene clarity and a quiet empowerment. Our clear thoughts guide our deeds. Our relaxed will supports our observations, contemplations and insights.

As we penetrate the soul mystery of equanimity, we will look at what inflames, agitates and disrupts our feelings. Emotions are the inflamers, agitators, and disruptors.

We are not to suppress our emotions. And we must never deny them. Emotions educate us. They keep us safe. They, most of all, challenge us to become self-aware and self-compassionate. They are the palette of colors that paint the portrait of our personalities, our relationships and our lifetimes.

In my study of emotions, I have recognized four basic ones: anger, fear, sadness and happiness. Many of my clients and students have asked "why only one positive emotion?" This is how emotional sabotage begins. Anger, fear and sadness are very positive. They teach us so much. They keep us awake and growing. If we only felt happiness, we would be fools and in danger. We would not question or observe or grow. We would be like plants. We would not need a soul or a future.

Revere all four emotions. Love your happiness, your anger, your sadness and your fear. If you reject or resent anger, fear and sadness, you will never know equanimity. Your life will not be a composition of self-love.

Our earthly existence is composed of these four emotions. The composition can be chaotic or calm. Embrace your four emotions - bring them into the light of self-compassion - and you will know equanimity and be able to accomplish your destiny with relative ease. Resist any of these emotions (and many of us reject happiness!) and your soul will suffer incompleteness. We embody our humanity when we embrace and manage all four emotions.

How do we manage our emotions? Equanimity arises when we give equal attention to each of the four emotions.

Pick an event in your life. Whether it is dramatic or mundane makes no difference. Tell the story of this event from each emotion. Tell it from anger, happiness, fear and sadness. Each story will be easy to tell from one or two emotions, one emotion will be difficult and one emotion will feel next to impossible. Yet this exercise will light the way to equanimity. Be willing to overcome the difficult and the impossible. If you expand your perception and response you will find your primary reaction is not the only reaction. You will find joy along side your suffering and suffering along side your joy.

You will begin to see that emotions can distract and delude or they can enhance and illuminate. If they are solo acts, they are destructive of your humanity. If they are all acknowledged equally, they are blessed friends awakening the gift of equanimity in your soul.

Just take today. Look at today with anger, with fear, with sadness and with happiness. Begin to see the full composition of your life with calmness. With calmness you will be able to call in the help of the spiritual world. If your energy is focused on resisting emotions, you will not be able to consciously experience the gifts of the spirit living in your unfolding life.

This is not an easy task. But if you succeed you will begin to own your emotions and they will stop owning you. Equanimity is the gateway to a sustained and confident presence of the Spirit.

THE NINTH HOLY NIGHT 2006/07

Your Soul's Tenth Quality
FECUNDITY

Rich, abundant productive fertility — this is the soul's fecundity. In our souls live all the creative forces and resources of spirit and matter. Our souls always have been and always will be fecund.

I have always been fascinated with the word, fecund. It fills me with the sense of overflowing possibility. But it also awakens questions in me about limitations and challenges.

Our souls' fecundity lives with both the frustration of limitations and challenges and the hunger for both. As we mature in our self-development, we learn consciously and willingly to set limitations and seek challenges to our fecundity.

Throughout our biographies, we can find numerous physical, emotional, social and economic restrictions, and confrontations, undermining our creative fulfillment. They appear to suck the wind out of our sails. Using your soul's quality of equanimity, make a short list of the limitations and challenges you have faced in your life this week. There will be reoccurring obstacles and onetime, out of the blue, events in this list. What pushes or holds you back? Consider where you feel frustrated, or even victimized, in your life's journey.

Meister Eckhart wisely said, "The true master is self-limiting." The self-limiting master is confident of the soul's fecundity and recognizes the necessity to make choices and set direction. Reflect on your life so far. Where have you designed the productivity of your soul? Have you shown the creative wisdom of an artist in shaping the richness of your life?

If you look at just today's limitations and challenges to your soul's fecundity, which were in your control and which were out of your control? Were you a master or a victim? A victim with equanimity can penetrate life's difficulties and find new knowledge of both the world and the soul, thus becoming a master. A master wisely and patiently unfolds his fruitfulness in the world.

Celebrate your soul's fecundity. Plan tomorrow's inner and outer activities. Discern your limitations and declare the challenges you will set for yourself. Then tomorrow evening review the unplanned challenges and limitations you found during the day. When you review your fruitfulness, look for both the spiritual, moral and the practical richness of your productivity. Both the planning, and the review, will strengthen your ability to bear fruit in the world.

Performing your daily review each evening is a beautiful discipline (whether you think it or write it). Choose one act during the course of the day and ask yourself what was true about the deed, what was beautiful about the deed and what was good about the deed. With practice this work develops the fecund presence of Spirit in all you do.

THE TENTH HOLY NIGHT 2006/07

Your Soul's Eleventh Quality
SAGACITY

As you have probably noticed every soul quality I have written about has ended with "ity." When I wrote these messages during the Holy Nights of 2006/7, deciding each day which quality to explore was a challenge. However, I trusted the fecundity of my soul and found both reason and inspiration supporting my choices. I wanted to delve into qualities that were not commonplace. I worked from a long list of "ity" soul qualities and trusted that each morning I would know which was calling to me to be explored.

For the eleventh message I chose to explore the mysteries of the soul quality sagacity. Sagacity is profound understanding, intimate knowing and acute judgment. As our journey in life takes us from innocence to wisdom, it is fitting to look into the quality of our soul's knowing.

Sagacity cannot be taught nor evaluated by others. We have the sacred texts and teachings that have come to us through the ages giving us profound models of wisdom. However, they are like a tricycle as compared to a bicycle. Where a rider is dependent on a tricycle to stay upright and balanced, uprightness and balance on a bicycle is dependent on the rider alone. Only you can discover the sagacity of your soul.

The quality of sagacity is not a study based on correctness or conformity. It is the quality of sudden recognition.

Curiously, sagacity is also defined as an acute sense of smell. Smell is a sudden perception. One moment an odor is there awakening your soul and then it fades with distance in time or space. Sagacity is not an accumulation of knowledge, it is the quality of knowing itself.

The soul's sagacity is moral discernment. The soul seeks out five ideals in all phenomena: Truth, Beauty, Goodness, Love and Freedom. These are not fixed, dictated ideals, not a set of standards developed to protect and prolong some political, cultural or religious world view. Rather, they are moral imaginations that are born in your soul as spirit and matter permeate each other within your personal consciousness.

Spend a few minutes imagining each of these five ideals. How do you recognize Truth, Beauty and Goodness? What is Love? What is Freedom? Do not be surprised if you find this meditation challenging or feel foolish and inarticulate. Most of us go through life without pondering these ideals.

Inner development and self-imagining expect a lot from us. They ask us to step beyond our normal thoughts and feelings. We must seek out higher meanings and perceptions. We commit to carry certain practices forward through the year.

Would you take some paper and write down each of these ideals in large letters or just type them in your word processing software and print them out? Be artistic in your rendering of the letters. Choose colors and fonts that express each ideal in some way. Hang these words where you will see them every day inspiring you to give them a moment's contemplation. Talk with a friend about these words.

Moral development does not occur without our attention. When you pay attention to ideals the spiritual world pays attention to you.

Sagacity is a surprising and momentary quality. It comes more frequently, when you have grown familiar with these five ideals.

THE ELEVENTH HOLY NIGHT 2006/07

Your Soul's Twelfth Quality
UNITY

The last soul quality, though it could well have been the first, is unity.

The soul makes one of many. It is the great container of infinite contexts. It holds all the many ways of being you together. It holds all the beginnings, middles and ends of you. It holds all the emotions and feelings, ideas and ideals, desires and disappointments, intentions and avoidances. It holds the doorways to the earthly and the spiritual. It's where your biography and biology in space and time meet your eternal divinity. It is where you find all your yes's, no's and maybe's.

A tiny magnet in the soul holds everything as one. It is a word. That word is "I." It is not quite a name. If I call out "I" no one would respond but me. My soul's name is "I". It is not Lynn. Lynn is my primary and formal name in space and time. I have lots of other names in space and time that signify different parts of me, or my life, or my relationships, or my work. "I" is the only signifier of all of me at all times in all ways. "I" is the unity of my individuality.

There is another unity dwelling in my soul. It is my humanity. My humanity unites me with everyone who has ever existed or ever will exist in time and space. All the people I know and don't know, those I like and don't like, those who believe in the same god or gods as I do and those who's gods have other names. My humanity is the soul that mirrors the sun shining on all of us throughout time. It is the other side of the unity coin in my soul, the universal experience of being human.

The unity coin is always being flipped. When I breathe in the coin flips to my individuality. When I breathe out it flips to my humanity. When I speak it flips to my individuality. When I listen it flips to my humanity.

What is important is not which side of the unity coin is facing up at any moment. It is being conscious of the two-sidedness of the coin.

When we are conscious, wise to the duality of our unity, life's journey reflects multi-dimensional love. With consciousness we can take the coin of unity and stand it on its side. Then we can take "unity" out of the horizontal and into a vertical gesture that reflects the soul as the bridge between spirit and matter. Now, give unity a spin. We all know that a flat circular coin spinning on its side looks like a sphere.

As a "sphere" our souls express the unity that exists between the self, the other, the spiritual and the earthly.

Spin some coins every day! Experience the fullness and completion of the qualities in your soul.

If man fully knows himself:

His self becomes the world;

If man fully knows the world:

The world becomes his self.*

*Rudolf Steiner

THE TWELFTH HOLY NIGHT 2006/07

157

158

The
Twelve Polarities
of Your Soul

The Gifts of Balancing

160

The gifts of the twelve polarities are the endless challenges for finding the right balance.

For each of us, the soul life, the sense of self, the path of inner development revolves around and evolves through our relationships to polarities. We orient our inner lives as we swing between the opposing poles. We long for one pole and resist the other. Or struggle with connecting to both, because both are equally essential.

Being human is about being bi-polar. But being human is also about the possibility of being balanced and centered while relating to both poles.

These messages were written during the Holy Nights 2007/08.

The Theme 2007/08

162

Your Soul's First Polarity
Solitude & Intimacy

Solitude and Intimacy is the polarity that holds us between uniting with ourselves and uniting with others. Some of us are more comfortable being by ourselves. Some of us are more comfortable being with others.

In solitude you are being with yourself by yourself. In intimacy you are with others and others are with you. Both solitude and intimacy are about "being with". "Being with" these are the two words that give meaning and purpose to solitude and intimacy.

Solitude and Intimacy are about "being with" in the gesture of transparency and vulnerability without losing your sense of integrity and authenticity. Transparency is to be seen completely with nothing hidden or altered. Vulnerability is the willing knowledge that you might be hurt by the other or disappointed in yourself. Vulnerability is also the capacity to grow and learn in both solitude and intimacy.

Our ability to know both the joy of solitude and the joy of intimacy is awakened by being compassionately revered by our caregivers in our earliest years. Through the mood of reverence we can be solitary and we can be intimate. When we lack being met with reverence in our early years we must learn to forgive others and ourselves and then to revere others and ourselves. The need to willfully birth reverence in our souls as adults because it was not planted in our young souls by our caregivers is common in our times. It may be the key challenge of our times.

Contemplating the relationships of "with self" and "with others" we find that both lead us to the spiritual feeling of being with God or with Spirit. The gift of solitude is discovering the Divine within. The gift of sacred intimacy is finding the Divine in the other.

Questions to Contemplate...

How do you imagine being with yourself as a sacred state? Do you see yourself fully and with a full and loving heart? Do you like being alone? Or is solitude an anxious state, a feeling of being in exile?

Do you seek intimacy with others because you lose your sense of aliveness if there is no one around to reflect your existence? Or do you find yourself most alive while alone?

How do you imagine being with others as a sacred state? Do you bring compassion to your seeing and hearing and feeling? Do you feel safe with intimacy? Do you have boundaries that breathe?

Do you know the intimate feeling of loving and being loved? Can you describe it? In being alone do you feel you are love?

How do you create the time and space for solitude?
For intimacy?

THE FIRST HOLY NIGHT 2007

Your's Soul's Second Polarity
Desire & Fulfillment

We call it our Christmas Wish List but it is a list of desires. We open our Christmas gifts hoping for fulfillment.

Solitude and Intimacy are poles of connecting. Desire and fulfillment are poles of longing – opposite, yet married to each other.

Without the experience of both the soul is incomplete. We have wonderful myths that speak to the horror of only knowing one pole. Narcissus and Echo is a story of only knowing desire. King Midas is a story of only knowing fulfillment.

Another picture of the necessity of both poles is in our breathing. We desire breath and inhale to know fulfillment. But if we hold our breath and don't exhale, we suffocate and die. So we exhale to create space for desire. Breathing is a wonderful expression of the essential dance between the pole of desire and the pole of fulfillment. Desire keeps the wheel of life turning. Fulfillment slows the wheel of life down – otherwise the turning of the wheel of life would develop such hysterical speed it would collapse.

We have the tendency to think of desire as the source of suffering and fulfillment as the source of joy. Is that true?

Desire relates us to the future. Fulfillment relates us to the past. We can move toward self-mastery and self-modulation if we reverse the relationship by asking two questions: What precedes the awakening of desire? What new desire will this fulfillment cause in my soul and create in my life?

The question living in desire is "What?" What do you desire? The question living in fulfillment is "How?" How is fulfillment achieved?

If you don't know what you desire, you will not know fulfillment. You will just suffer with an unnamed desire. Nameless desire is a horrible thing. But maybe you are afraid to name your desire. Maybe you have too many desires to name.

If you do not know how to acquire fulfillment, you will suffer with the increasing burden of unmet desires. If you are too focused on what you desire and not focused on how you will achieve fulfillment – your life will weigh in heavily on desire. You want to keep the scale between the thought of desire and the intention to fulfill balanced. Do you keep a balance?

There is a core part of our being that is pure spirit, a kernel of the Divine. In the realms of spirit, there is no experience of the polarity of desire and fulfillment. Desire and fulfillment are one in those realms. If you can experience or observe your life from this divine part of your being, you will know peace in desire and peace in fulfillment while actively desiring and actively fulfilling.

Questions to Contemplate...

Obviously, the key work is to make these thoughts personal – to wake them up in your daily life and to ask the questions about "what" and "how."

What do you desire? Make a list and make it very specific. I often ask my clients to write a list of 100 very specific *"I desire"* statements. It is very difficult.

How do you fulfill each desire? Make a list of all the how questions and all the people you might ask to help you figure it out.

Did anyone ever mentor you in recognizing your desires and going for them?

THE SECOND HOLY NIGHT 2007

Your Soul's Third Polarity
Movement & Stillness

The polarity of Movement and Stillness brings us to our experience of action.

Our souls have three functions — thinking, feeling and willing. When we sleep, our souls work to renew our thinking, rebalance our feeling and restore our willing. Willing is the soul impulse that proceeds all action. As we explore the polarity of Activity — movement and stillness — we are bringing more awareness to our will.

I have written in my brief Inner Christmas Bio, about the profound and wonderful influence of Rudolf Steiner on my life and work. Dr. Steiner designed the curriculum and pedagogy of

Waldorf education. Both my children went to the Waldorf School of Princeton. Through being a Waldorf mom, I learned most of the fundamental foundation of what I share in the Inner Christmas Messages. Waldorf reveres the child and her developing functions of the Head (Thinking), the Heart (Feeling) and the Hand (Willing).

Becoming aware of movement and stillness in our thinking, feeling and willing will (!) awaken a new power in our lives. It will give us the power to manage our motives and our activities.

Stillness holds more mystery for me. Stillness is more primal than movement. Stillness is the source of movement, not just its other pole. Absolute stillness holds the potential for infinite movement.

Stillness is the absence of personal rhythm ... and the presence of harmonic resonance with the Spirit. You are empty of your own motives and filled with the Universe. Many individuals spend lifetimes of meditation seeking this stillness. Others are blessed with moments of stillness without any intention or anticipation.

Healthy, beautiful movement is supported by the alternation of personal rhythms with cosmic rhythms. This is most visible in great dancers and great athletes. They are so unique and so universal in their movements. Some spend lifetimes in movement development and others find it in a momentary surprise.

We need awareness of rhythm as we come to recognize the polarity of stillness and movement. It is very difficult to be still and not move when you hear and feel a strong beat. Conversely, stillness is easier — and movement more difficult — when there is no demanding beat.

Habitual movement is dead movement for with habitual movement the soul is no longer penetrating movement with meaning or purpose. Our habitual movements are machine-like. They have neither personal rhythm nor cosmic rhythm living in them. In our modern times, with so many repetitive movements that we want to do automatically, we have a growing interest in forms of conscious movement like yoga and tai chi. Does this possibly show the presence of something divine within our soul seeking to remedy the deadening patterns of modern culture?

In stillness we can remain immobile or begin to move. Many of us struggle with movement or stillness when the alarm clock shouts "Move!" and our bodies cry "Still!"

With stillness we can consider two verbs: to still and to stay still — consciously to stop moving or not to start moving. Both become easier with attention to our inner relationship to stillness and movement.

Again, memories of childhood can illuminate our attention. Parents either forget or lack patience for the incredibly fascinating challenge of childhood living in movement. Consequently, in our will we find inhibiting emotional echoes of the parental demands of "Stay still!" or "Get moving!

Time to move to the questions ... or perhaps, you need a moment or two of stillness before moving on.

Questions to Contemplate...

There is something so serene in the thought of stillness and something so poetic in the verb "to still." How do you still your thinking? That is not put your thinking to sleep, but willfully still it. Do you have moments of stillness? Do you want to still your thoughts? What about your feelings? If you are a workaholic, do you need to still your will?

Imagine graceful movement. Can you spend time contemplating what it takes to initiate movement from the place of stillness? Grace is movement flowing with the force of stillness.

How do you initiate a new thought? How does movement appear in your thinking? And not through prejudice, fantasy or addiction. Through joy? Through enthusiasm? Through suffering? Through love?

What rhythms in your life support the actions you take?

Does an inner command to "Be still" create a sense of safety or danger? What about an inner command to "Get moving"?

Here is a poem that says it all. It is by Wendell Berry from The Country of Marriage, 1973

> *Willing to die,*
> *you give up*
> *your will, keep still*
> *until, moved*
> *by what moves*
> *all else, you move.*

THE THIRD HOLY NIGHT 2007

Your Soul's Fourth Polarity
Vertical & Horizontal

Vertical and horizontal are the poles that describe the two gestures of being human. We live in the vertical as beings bridging between spirit and matter. We live in the horizontal as we engage in and with the world. Together they form a cross, one of the earliest symbols of human understanding. To explore the meaning in each of these poles we must understand the cross. To understand the cross we must penetrate the meaning and representation of proportion.

There is a very good description of the symbol of the cross on www.Wikipedia.com. You may want visually to explore the images of the cross to develop your feeling for the poles of the horizontal and the vertical.

When we seek the vertical pole in our souls we are looking for our right relationship to spirit and matter. We are born into this life to incarnate fully. We want to engage fully with the weight of gravity. We need to feel our feet on the ground and have access to all the energies emanating from Mother Earth.

At the same time, we must fully connect to the inner experience of our original divinity and the pole of spirit, the lightness of levity, the open reaches of the heavens and the inspirations of the gods.

It is through the vertical pole that we can materialize spirit and spiritualize matter. It measures our spiritual development and our practical achievements.

The horizontal pole represents our relationship to others and participation in the world through perceptions, interests and experiences.

A horizon is a meeting or a boundary between two separate thoughts, feelings, entities or realities as known through our perceptions, our interests and our experiences. It is important to bring our attention to meaning and to the influence of the horizon. Go outside and look at the horizon of the sky and earth. You are viewing the sense perceptible mirror of the reality of spirit meeting matter.

The vertical and horizontal poles become visible in the image of the cross. And the point where the poles cross makes visible the relationship of self to everything else through proportion.

Ideal proportion creates beauty.

There is no beauty when the arms of the cross are not proportional. Proportion is based on the proportions of the human body and is found in the Golden Section. Proportion based on the Golden Section is not about equal proportions, it is about a beautiful ratio of one aspect to the other. Pythagoras, the great Greek initiate, said, "The Human Being is the measure of all things." All the great temples, cathedrals, pyramids and places of spiritual importance are designed as a reflection of the proportions of the human body. This is why these structures feel sacred. Each human being is a temple and feels sacred when the proportions of the crossing of the vertical and horizontal poles inwardly and outwardly express the Golden Section.

Each human being needs to find the right proportions, the beautiful horizons, of their souls and their lifetimes as they dwell in the vertical between spirit and matter.

The Golden Mean as a philosophical experience is the recognition and understanding of deficiency and excess. Beauty is destroyed by excess and deficiency. The soul through consciousness of the polarity of vertical and horizontal is able to seek, create and restore proportion. This is the path of moral development...the right proportion at the right time for the circumstances.

Questions to Contemplate...

The polarity between the horizontal and the vertical lead us to many considerations and contemplations that are rich with self-knowledge and self-development.

Begin with the vertical pole between spirit and matter. Where on this pole is your horizon? Where does your spiritual sky meet your material earth? Have you fully incarnated into your earthiness? Do you appreciate it? Or do you lean to the spiritual and disdain the material. Nothing is more beautiful than fully incarnated spirit. If we resist spirit or resist matter, we do not express right proportion.

Now into the horizontal? List some horizontal relationships. For example, how do you relate to obedience and rebellion, work and rest, art and science, age and youth, giving and receiving, speaking and listening? Do you prefer the excess of one and the deficiency of the other? Remember to consider your perceptions, your interests and your experience.

Do you perceive one more clearly than the other?

Do you have more interest in one than the other?

Do you have more experience with one than the other?

Every day pay attention to proportion in all things. Keep a journal of proportion. Draw crosses. As you review your days draw the vertical and horizontal poles. Be truthful and compassionate in where you place the crossing point. You will be all the wiser for this attention and your ability to perceive beauty, to create beauty and to sustain beauty in your thoughts, your feelings and your deeds will increase proportionately.

THE FOURTH HOLY NIGHT 2007

Your Soul's Fifth Polarity
FREEDOM & LAWFULNESS

In working (thinking, reflecting, questioning, writing) with polarities, I find myself with three choices:

Work with one.

Work with the other one.

Work with the relationship of the two.

These choices often leave me frozen and intimidated. Eventually, I just jump and see where I land. I suggest you work with them this way, too. You really can't go wrong. The only wrong is staying frozen.

I will begin with lawfulness and then work with freedom. There are two types of lawfulness - Creative and Arbitrary.

Creative lawfulness is a beautiful experience. The laws make sense from all perspectives. They fit the situation, the process, the problem or the opportunity. They allow, rather than prohibit. They protect, rather than persecute. They distinguish, rather than collapse.

Nature is based on creative lawfulness. Consequently, Nature is harmonious. It works.

Arbitrary lawfulness is distorting and destructive. These laws only make sense to those who are ambitious, arrogant or frightened. They are based on disharmony, elitism and entitlement. They punish, rather than redeem. They inhibit, rather than encourage.

Our bodies and souls contain both forms of lawfulness. Every human body has laws that are creative and laws that are arbitrary. Think of the laws of digestion, reproduction, cognition, mobility, etc. Body laws can be harmonious and bless us with well-being or they can feel arbitrary and inconvenient causing struggle and discomfort.

The two forms of lawfulness shape our souls with instincts, attitudes, reactions, pain and pleasure. Creative laws support stability, security and sanity and allow for mobility, flexibility and possibility. Arbitrary soul laws support prejudice, fantasy and addiction.

Freedom is indefinable as it lives in the spirit of the individual. Freedom is not about laws. Freedom is beyond all laws.

Do not confuse rights with freedom, Rights are prerogatives and privileges. Do not confuse independence with freedom. Independence is the denial of dependence on the laws of others. Do not confuse liberty and rebellion with freedom. Liberty and rebellion are about not having to obey or rejecting all laws.

Freedom is what stands behind creative laws, rights, independence, liberty and rebellion. If we penetrate our laws, rights, independence, liberty and rebellion, we will find a feeling for freedom.

Freedom is a spiritual state. Spirit is never not free. When Spirit fully incarnates it is experienced as freedom.

Freedom is not surrounded by emotions, not even happiness. Happiness appears when life conforms to our personal laws or our desired laws.

Freedom is always present, but not always known. Freedom is always true, beautiful and good. Freedom is never measured or qualified. It is all or nothing.

Freedom is eternal and momentary. We glimpse freedom in moment of grace. We cannot capture freedom nor hold on to it.

We can believe in freedom with our thoughts. We can be open to freedom in our feeling. We can strive for freedom in our will. When we think, feel or act in freedom something beyond extraordinary has come through us.

To live our earthly lives we need lawfulness. To give meaning to our earthly lives we need freedom.

Questions to Contemplate...

Clearly, we want to question our own personal laws. If we ask the right questions with courage, reverence and compassion, freedom will answer.

Write down all your laws — the good, the bad and the ugly laws. Some will be obvious to you and some will be very subtle. Try to uncover a couple of the subtle laws. The list will be endless, so just begin with 12. Now look at which of the 12 feel creative or feel arbitrary.

Consider how these laws relate to your rights, your independence, your liberty and your rebellion.

You can rewrite some laws and write off others. Some laws will feel just right.

When we relate objectively to our own personal laws, we can effectively question our political, social and religious laws.

To glimpse freedom, write a poem, dance, sing with the birds.

THE FIFTH HOLY NIGHT 2007

Your Soul's Sixth Polarity
WARMING & COOLING

After the profound work of Freedom and Lawfulness in the last message, I hope the polarity of Warming and Cooling brings some gentle calming to our souls.

Warming and cooling are such comforting gestures.

To comfort is to restore strength. There are draining situations in life when we find being warmed or cooled provides new strength. This is the strength of the temperate middle. There are times when we find strength in the warm light of day. Other times strength comes in the cool of night.

We warm or cool to restore the harmony in the body's temperature and to the soul's temperament. "Temper," as a root, means to mingle elements in order to moderate.

Temper also means to tune a piano as Bach reminds us in "The Well-Tempered Clavier."

Warming and cooling are the ways we:

- Comfort our bodies and souls,

- Harmonize and moderate our bodies and souls, and

- Tune our bodies and souls in order to make beautiful music with our individuality and our humanity.

As we imagine warming and cooling, we need also to imagine being too hot or too cold. We only need warming when we have become too cold and cooling when we have become too hot.

Bathing and breathing are the two most natural ways we cool down and warm up our bodies. With both bathing and breathing we can restore our perfect temperature. With breathing no matter how hot or cold the air is as soon as we inhale the air conforms to our body temperature. Depending on our need, a few moments in a warm or cool bath will bring our bodies to a comfortable temperature.

Through soul breathing we can alter the temperature of our environment. Through bathing our soul with the ideals of truth, beauty, goodness and compassion we can warm or cool our thoughts, our feelings and our intentions.

Questions to Contemplate...

Does your soul respond to physical, emotional or spiritual stress by turning cold and sclerotic or getting overheated and inflamed? What spiritual comforting do you seek to warm up your coldness or cool down your inflammation?

As a personality do you tend towards the heated emotions of happiness and anger or are your impulses chilled by fear and sadness? How do you temper or moderate a one-sided personality?

If you were to imagine yourself as a piano, do you need tuning? Do your tones need warming or cooling? What will allow you to strike the right tone on your life path?

How do you tune your soul? How do you moderate your

personality? How do you create the right soul temperature to allow you to thrive as a spiritual being and an earthly being?

Who in your life warms you up? Who in your life cools you down?

Can you spend a few moments imagining your restorative metaphors for soul breathing and soul bathing?

Some additional thoughts on the Work of the Holy Nights Messages...

The Messages ask us to think, think deeply and openly. During this sacred work, we think with our hearts, not our heads. Our hearts maintain the perfect temperature for calm thinking — a balance between spirit and matter.

Here is the verse Rudolf Steiner wrote for Christmas week in his book, Calendar of the Soul. I find it expresses the purpose of the Holy Nights' messages and the activity of the thinking of the heart.

Surrendered to the spirit's revelation,

I win back the light of cosmic being.

It grows and grows,

enlightening me,

to give my self back to me.

And this feeling of my self---

awakening ---

unravels itself

out of my strength

as a thinker.

Translated by Tom Mellett.

Did you do a little unraveling around warming and cooling tonight?

THE SIXTH HOLY NIGHT 2007

Your Soul's Seventh Polarity
Reflection & Anticipation

For this last night of our measured year, knowing that at the midnight hour a new measured year begins. I want to explore how we relate to what has been and what will become. Tonight we will reflect and anticipate.

Reflection comes from the Latin word that means to bend back. "Bend" has such grace in its meaning. When we reflect in our thinking we gracefully bend back to what was past. Reflection is not analysis or evaluation which are often unbending. Reflection is filled with heart.

We reflect on any period of time and the thoughts, feelings and deeds that filled that time with meaning. We reflect on emotions and relationships. We reflect on the "yes's", the "no's" and the "maybe's" of the past.

Reflect on all that has passed by, all that has metamorphosed, all that has remained the same or stood still. Bend back again and again and feel the vitality of the experience.

Note the lovely mood of the recall during reflection. Call out to what has happened in the past year. Call out to all those with whom you spent time with, spoke to and listened to. Call out to who you were then and listen to the echo of your old way of being. Even when reflection finds pain or regret, if we remain in our soft bending heart we will find comfort.

Knowing that we are on a spiritual journey between the threshold of birth and the threshold of death, when we reflect, we might genuflect with reverence in our times of reflection. Genuflect with your body and your soul.

With reflection we bend back.
With anticipation we bend forward.

Anticipation is found in expectation and in preparation. As we think of tomorrow, next year or whenever, we need to anticipate wisely.

Through anticipation we confront the requirements for meeting and shaping the future. We can picture how the future will shape our lives. We can be aware of what is coming toward us.

When we anticipate, we lean toward the future with soft strength. We can meet the good with enthusiasm and the bad with courage. Without anticipation, we are naïve and shallow about the future and we are at risk to overlook the good and to be trampled by the bad.

Neither reflection nor anticipation is healthy if we resist the truth of the past or the future. Nor are they healthy if we reflect or anticipate from only one perspective.

Remember, the bend is significant. Reflect and anticipate as if you were moving around a bend and seeing both the past and the future from a moving point of view.

Questions to Contemplate…

First, find the bending reflective path in your heart.

Second, look back on the previous year. What events are large and filled with meaning? What events seemed large but now, on reflection are small and without significant meaning? With each event do you feel gratitude or resentment?

Now look at yourself in each event. What do you see? Describe yourself as you were? Why did this event occur? What did it move you toward?

Third, from the same bending path in your heart, look in the direction of the future. What is coming toward you? Are you preparing for these anticipated events? How will you respond to the developing future? Are you willing to change?

You might write your "past self" a letter of reflection and your "future self" a letter of anticipation.

THE SEVENTH HOLY NIGHT 2007

Your Soul's Eighth Polarity
GATHERING & SPREADING

Human Beings stand upright. No animal stands upright. Anatomically this uprightness is possible through the design of our pelvis, but its purpose is to free our arms and our hands for certain creative gestures and deeds.

Spend a moment or two relating to your arms and your hands and their freedom. Think about how you use your arms and hands to create and to express yourself, not just to meet your survival needs. Feel the flow of directing and empowering energy coming from your heart into your gathering and spreading arms. Feel this energy right out to the tips of your fingers.

I smile as I contemplate this polarity of gathering and spreading. The reason for the smile lies in the heart force that lives in both poles. When I imagine gathering and spreading, I see my arms and my hands contracting into my heart and expanding out from my heart.

Your heart gathers and your heart spreads. Your physical heart gathers in from the body with venal blood and spreads out to the body with arterial blood. But our focus here is on the gathering and spreading forces of your spiritual heart.

The spiritual heart gathers in the spiritual world to spread in the material world. But it also gathers in the material world to spread in the spiritual world. The first statement most of us will naturally understand. However, the idea that we gather in the material world for spreading in the spiritual world calls for thought. How does that occur?

The beings of the spiritual world, from the angels to the seraphim, have continuously poured their forces into earthly existence and human hearts. How do we return that gift? We return these gifts through meditation, prayer, silence and reflection. In all these acts we offer up to the spiritual world our forces of love. In addition, we bring to spiritual beings the perceptions of the temporal world that we gather with our senses. When we experience beauty, kindness, compassion and moral freedom we gather earthly goodness into our souls and we spread that goodness in the spiritual world. We do our gathering during our waking hours, and when we enter spiritual realities through the threshold of sleep, we begin to spread our earthly love among those beings that love us.

After we spread our earthly love, we are now empty and able to gather new spiritual gifts. And so when we awake in the morning filled with new spiritual gifts, we begin to spread this spiritual love out to the world through our thoughts, feelings and actions.

We gather love and we spread love.
We must gather and spread wisely.

Questions to contemplate…

How do you pay attention to what you gather and what you spread?

Do you attend to what you perceive with your senses? Can you go to bed tonight and gather all the temporal riches of tastes, smells, textures, sounds and sights you experienced during the day? Can you release all that lacks beauty before you fall into sleep?

Can you gather your centering, balancing, harmonizing capacities for your review of the day? Do you pray, meditate and recall the subtle moments and gestures of kindness and compassion that you found in your daily life?

Do you spend time reading poetry or literature or writing words of meaning? What about experiences of music, sculpture, dance and other arts?

In your world of work, do you think about what you gather and what you spread?

In your relationships, what do you pour into the hearts of those you interact with? What do they pour into you? And don't forget to remember the face of a passing stranger?

May you be blessed by what you gather
and bless with what you spread.

THE EIGHTH HOLY NIGHT 2006/07

Your Soul's Ninth Polarity
Asleep & Awake

The polarity of Asleep & Awake requires such wakeful attention. Don't let your soul go to sleep as you contemplate this message.

Sleep restores. Wakefulness exhausts. How do you let your soul rest? How do you let your soul dream?

Sleep avoids. Wakefulness attends. What do you naturally attend to with rich wakefulness? What calls out for your attention that you want to avoid? Does your soul run away? Does in run toward?

Sleep is dull even clueless. Wakefulness is alert and on the mark. Oh, how do we see our soul's bored with our sense perceptions, our repetitive questions, the lack of wisdom and love. How do we celebrate the sudden visit to our soul of truth, beauty or goodness?

Without sleep, we would never be awake. Without wakefulness, we would not need sleep. Life would not be a conscious experience or a creative one. There would be no sense of self and no sense of spirit if this polarity did not exist.

When your soul is awake to yourself, it is asleep to the soul of others. When you soul is awake to the soul of another, it is asleep to itself. It is in this social gesture that we need to be aware of our proportions and can imagine this as a *pas de deux*, the elegant balance of solos when two dancers are sharing the stage. Sometimes we need to remain awake more to ourselves or more to others but we should not neglect our need for one pole or the other.

The soul can be awake to earthly realities and to spiritual realities, but not at the same time. When we are awake to earthly realities we are asleep to spiritual realities and vice versa.

We must look at how we are awake or asleep in our thinking.

If we fall asleep in our thinking, our will can become compulsive. If we fall asleep in our will, our thinking can become obsessive. And our feeling life if too awake or too asleep will lead us into madness.

If we pay attention to the movement of the soul between being asleep and being awake, we become more sensitive to the creative possibilities living in consciousness.

Questions to contemplate…

When you contemplate or focus your thoughts, feelings or activities on earthly realms, even the beauty of nature, acts of kindness, or thoughts of deep meaning do you notice a point when your soul feels weary?

Do you ever experience restlessness, longing or eagerness in your soul? Do you need to wake up or put to sleep your thinking, feeling or willing?

Are you resistant to being awake to yourself or awake to others. So many feel be awake to others is more holy than being awake to yourself. Do you think you can really understand others if you never wakeup to your individuality?

How long can you stay awake in your thinking?

Have you ever heard a soul snore??? I know this seem irreverent but if you think about it there is a sensitivity to the presence and functions of soul that can tell if another soul is awake, dreaming or snoring/sleeping.

Then there is the nodding soul that is neither awake nor asleep.

A soul that expresses itself sentimentally or cynically is not awake...it just gives the appearance of being awake. This soul needs to go to sleep and rest so that freedom and love can be restored and the direct experience of truth, beauty and goodness can be refreshed.

Now ask yourself how the right balance between asleep and awake makes a life of sweet dreams come true.

THE NINTH HOLY NIGHT 2007/08

Your Soul's Tenth Polarity
Leading & Following

Now we go ballroom dancing. The dance floor is our soul. The music is our destiny. The dance floor is filled with couples — all the polarities we have been working with.

I have worked with ballroom dancing as a metaphor for healthy relationships often. It is important and lovely to think of all the polarities of our inner life as dancing partnerships.

The other metaphor for the interaction within polarity is the battleground. It is not surprising that in a time of war and terror, ballroom dancing has become a cultural fascination. The dance floor and the battleground are opposites and opposites attract!

The reason the dance floor is so opposite to the battleground in the peaceful polar presence of leading and following. If we do not understand the gifts of this dancing polarity, all other polarities will find themselves at war rather than moving to the music.

On the battleground leaders dominate and followers submit. The poles, in constant imbalance, exaggerate their difference and create a destructive soul life. On the dance floor, leaders are responsible and followers responsive. Both poles enhance each other and enrich the soul.

BallroomDancers.com has a learning center that is full of insight on successful leading and following. These insights are worth considering as metaphors for the healthy, creative dancing of the polarities of your soul.

Both dancers need TONE. Tone is strength. If one pole is weak, the dancing is awkward and unbalanced. It takes strength to lead and to follow.

Both dancers need to be ACTIVE. Each pole needs energetic vitality and the ability to transmit and receive signals. An active pole creates an electric pulse or tension between leading and following. The poles breathe life into each other.

Both dancers need MUTUAL AWARENESS. There is a sensitive and subtle conversation going on between leader and follower at all times.

Ballroom dancing teaches us that leading and following have nothing to do with dominance and submission and everything to do with harmonious action and reaction. The lead determines the rhythm, the direction, and the steps. The follower must maintain a slight resistance to the lead creating a vibrant tension. The follower responds with a magical sensitivity which makes two appear as one. This is the gift, genius and miracle of the polarity of leading and following, the two appear as one.

Becoming one requires practice, patience, perseverance and forgiveness. The concordant outcome of strong leading and strong following is an elegant and graceful dancing soul.

Questions to Contemplate...

Understanding the polarity of leading and following in the frame of a dancing couple appearing as one empowers us to lead or follow comfortably in all kinds of life situations. Think of a few situations where you were resistant to or had difficulty with either leading or following. Why?

Play some leading and following games with a willing friend or colleague. Follow their movements for five minutes. Discuss the experience. Now reverse the leading and following roles. Discuss. You will learn something new about your experience of leading and following every time. Life in the world and in your soul will become more peaceful and creative.

Now explore the polarity of leading and following as it functions in all the other polarities in your soul life. Do the other polarities dance as one? Are some polarities into domination and submission?

Are the poles equally strong? If one is weak and submissive, can you give it some extra attention? Was this pole wounded or abandoned in your life? Is one pole a dominant bully - always demanding your soul's attention? Consider the reasons for one-sidedness in any polarity.

Imagine a conversation between the poles.
Write the conversation down in your journal.

Watch Fred Astaire movies and Dancing With the Stars.

THE TENTH HOLY NIGHT 2007/08

Your Soul's Eleventh Polarity
Passion & Compassion

Passion and Compassion are another polarity that relates to the heart.

I want a heart that is both passionate and compassionate. Passion and compassion have to do with joy and suffering in earthly and spiritual realms. To feel one and not the other would lead to a very lopsided life.

Passion arises in the earthly, selfish heart wanting heavenly joy through earthly experience. It is the feeling of intense enthusiasm, demanding hunger, or painful longing.

Passion fills our souls with self-interest and drives us to self-fulfillment and self-satisfaction. Passion's selfishness is necessary. It is a joyful expression of individuality.

Sadly, passion can become inflamed, obsessive and never be satisfied. Uncontrolled passion brings suffering to the soul. Passion lives in a balanced metamorphosis between the force of arousal and the release through satisfaction. Passion can flame out in unrelieved arousal or die stillborn in apathy.

We need to find our passions and to know them well. We can share the ideas that are shaped by our passions and we can engage others in the deeds that fulfill our passions.

However, as an emotional feeling, our passions are a solitary experience. We feel only with ourselves.

Compassion is different. It is the other side of passionate feeling — the side that is not "by myself" but "with the other." Compassion is the heart of the spiritual heart.

Compassion is the sharing of feeling. Compassion is not shared ideas, imaginations, or visions. Compassion is not the sharing of intentions or deeds. It is simply and purely shared feeling.

There is no selfishness in compassion. To experience the feeling of another, we must die to our own feeling, die to our own passions. "Thy feeling, not mine." We find we suffer another's suffering and we rejoice in another's joy. There is something humanly divine in the experience of compassion.

However, we must thoughtfully choose compassion. Compassion is the intense awakening to the needs of the other, not the awakening of one's own needs. To have your feelings overtaken by the feelings of another, unconsciously, is dangerous and shows a lack of boundaries and self-protection. Compassion is a conscious and willed love. With the "with-ness" of compassion, we become one through *dis*passionate love.

A synonym for dispassion is "composed." How do we live a life composed of passion and compassion?

Let us strive dispassionately to be compassionately passionate and passionately compassionate.

Questions to Contemplate...

Write down twelve passions. Revel in your selfish delights and cravings. Do not hold back. Do not cool down your heat. Go to the extreme end of this pole.

Over the coming days, weeks, months explore these passions. Finely draw their images and plan to execute the necessary actions to fulfill these passions. Are they practical or impractical? Whose help will you need?

Do these passions give your life meaning? Do you suffer because of them. Which of them become the torture of an itch that can't be scratched?

Now go to the pole of compassion. Whose feelings do you bear in your heart? Whose feelings do you reject? Do you ever feel another's feelings as if they had taken over your life? How can you establish your freedom?

Have you thought about what it means to know another's feelings?

This contemplation will strengthen your humanity and your individuality. From the place of dispassion love is a free choice.

THE ELEVENTH HOLY NIGHT 2007/08

Your Soul's Twelfth Polarity
Certainty & Doubt

I have chosen certainty and doubt as the closing couple. How do we marry certainty and doubt in our souls? For me these two are hopelessly and wonderfully intertwined in my soul.

Certainty comforts me. It tells me I am experiencing what is true. True for me in the moment.

Moment is my favorite measure of time. A moment can be indefinably brief or it can take forever depending on the thought, feeling or action that occupies it.

So certainty is a feeling found in moments filled with truth, confidence and elegance.

Yet, I am wary of lasting certainty and its comfort. Lasting certainty seductively asks me to fly high like Icarus, forgetting that my wings are held together with wax and that the sun is hot. Let certainty be momentary … and tempered by wisdom.

Wisdom in her wariness will ask questions of certainty: How close can I fly to the sun before melting? Do I need a parachute? Wisdom knows the dangers of lasting certainty. Answer her questions.

Doubt challenges me. It tells me that my reality, spiritual or earthly, is complex and fluid. Doubt gives me choices: I can float or drown. Yes, doubt is watery.

I work to make friends with doubt. I can float in our friendship. When I experience doubt as an enemy, I sink to the bottomless bottom of my soul and drown.

Wisdom urges me to form a lasting friendship with doubt. Be certain of doubt.

Last, make balanced lovers of certainty and doubt. You want to marry them. Your soul is blessed by both of them. If we marry certainty with doubt, we gain an excellent pair of poles to move us forward in our growth and development. The marriage will be challenged by the presence of" right and wrong" or "arrogance and modesty." Think of these pairs as warring in-laws. Keep them safely away from certainty and doubt.

Like all polarities, your soul may know one pole more than the other. Which pole are you more familiar with? Do you swim often with doubt or go flying with certainty? Are you afraid of flying? Did you ever learn how to float?

Confidence is what marries certainty and doubt and takes them safely flying and swimming in the realms of spirit and matter. Confidence is the supporting element that asks questions of certainty and speaks statements to doubt.

Celebrate both certainty and doubt.

Questions to Contemplate...

Give yourself permission to be both certain and doubtful for these exercises.

Make a list of twelve things about which you are certain. Make a spiritual list and an earthly list. Make a list of thoughts, feelings and results of deeds about which you are certain.

Choose a few and start writing down the doubts you would have if you weren't certain. Pay attention.

Now make the list of doubts. What makes you certain of these doubts? How do these doubts serve you? If a particular doubt disappeared, what would your life look like?

Ask how doubtful you are of the items on your certain lists and how certain you are about those on your doubt lists. Notice the convergence.

THE TWELFTH HOLY NIGHT 2007/08

221

222

224

SUBSCRIBE

to receive this year's

INNER CHRISTMAS MESSAGES

during the Holy Nights

You will receive links to the messages and
be able to participate in the Inner Christmas Community forum.

http://imagineself.com/icm-subscribe/

226

My Note of Gratitude

My heart is full of gratitude for all the wonderful people that have supported and encouraged me as I have put together this book. As I think about them, I feel my whole being smile.

I would like to name all of them, but it would take longer to write than the book as I would drift into a reverie of thoughts about each one. Perhaps one day I will post on my website a gratitude page with all the names and descriptions of the love they gave me. What a happy idea.

To all my subscribers, many who have been with me for years, I want to say thank you.

There are certain people whose generosity of time and talent has been extraordinary. They made the book happen. I am listing them alphabetically, a neutral order.

The guys that through the years have supported my work through creative conversations and amazing efforts.
John Beck
Edward Schuldt
Alan Shalleck

The women who have consistently offered the incredible gifts of devoted friendship, loving patience, sound advice and supportive enthusiasm. I can't imagine life without them. They hold my heart and edit my words.
Ruth Boulter
Peg Carmody
Mandy Sutton
Chocolate Waters

These men and women have been at my back. They have listened to my crazy struggles. They have kept me grounded. They have edited, suggested and celebrated the messages. Words fail the love and gratitude I feel.

Reading is a visual experience and Lee Hannam has designed this book with careful thought and incredible talent. Working with her is a joy. She is truly an artist.

Two individuals bless my life always - my daughter, Thea, and my son, Lucian. I love you. Thank you and your spouses, Sokol and Sonja, for my grandchildren.

Finally, I want to acknowledge Rudolf Steiner (1861-1925). His living wisdom about all things spiritual, human and material is the inspirational foundation on which my thoughts stand.

ABOUT THE AUTHOR
LYNN JERICHO

Lynn's birth announcement was a Christmas card as she was born in a blizzard on December 11. Writing the Inner Christmas Messages was her destiny. ;-)

For her whole life, Lynn has thought deeply about and been devoted to the meanings and mysteries of being human and struggled to cultivate the direct experience, the conscious imagination and the articulated sense of self, the I Am, in herself and in others.

She is fearless, radical, clear and compassionate in her work as a writer, speaker and mentor.

"I love the Holy Nights. Every morning I wake up knowing I must write an Inner Christmas message that thousands of people around the world will be reading in a few hours. Since the first message of Inner Christmas, I have felt humble and surprised, while also feeling so right. My joy at Christmas is complete and I am so grateful."

To learn more about Lynn: **www.imagineself.com/about-Lynn/**

THE IMAGINE SELF ACADEMY

Besides Inner Christmas, Lynn has developed many online self-directed courses for awakening new imaginations of yourself, of being human, of the future and of spirituality. The courses fall into five curriculums:

Core Imaginations focus on understanding who you are and what it means to be human.

Holy Imaginations offer self-development from a new Esoteric Christian perspective.

Wisdom Imaginations provide creative insights for healing, liberating and empowering your individuality.

Destiny Imaginations address the conscious unfolding of your future.

Karmic Imaginations guide you in recollecting your life story.

Learn more: www.imagineself.com

Lynn also offers private mentoring, coaching and listening. She gives talks and workshops in many places around the world.

Contact her: lynnjericho@gmail.com

Made in the USA
Columbia, SC
12 December 2017